"POWERFUL WORDS, THOUGHTS AND INSPIRATIONS FOR THE SOUL"

DR. SHARON C. CASON

authorHOUSE®

AuthorHouse™
1663 Liberty Drive
Bloomington, IN 47403
www.authorhouse.com
Phone: 1 (800) 839-8640

Published by AuthorHouse   09/07/2017

ISBN: 978-1-5246-5085-8 (sc)
ISBN: 978-1-5246-5083-4 (hc)
ISBN: 978-1-5246-5084-1 (e)

Library of Congress Control Number: 2016919254

Print information available on the last page.

Scripture quotations marked NIV are taken from the Holy Bible, New
International Version®. NIV®. Copyright © 1973, 1978, 1984 by International
Bible Society. Used by permission of Zondervan. All rights reserved. [Biblica]

Scripture quotations marked NLT are taken from the Holy Bible, New Living
Translation, copyright © 1996, 2004, 2007. Used by permission of Tyndale House
Publishers, Inc. Carol Stream, Illinois 60188. All rights reserved. Website

Scripture quotations marked KJV are from the Holy Bible, King James Version
(Authorized Version). First published in 1611. Quoted from the KJV Classic
Reference Bible, Copyright © 1983 by The Zondervan Corporation.

INTRODUCTION

In 2012, I began a weekly radio ministry called Powerful Living Ministry. Messages of joy, hope and comfort were sent over the air ways to bless whoever tuned in.

Now the Holy Spirit has prompted me to place these messages in book form so that many more may be blessed, encouraged and healed by the living, breathing and powerful Word of God.

Whether written of spoken, the Word of God is, according to Hebrews 4:12… *"quick, and powerful, and sharper than any two-edged sword, piercing even to the dividing asunder of soul and spirit, and of the joints and marrow, and is a discerner of the thoughts and intents of the heart." (KJV)*

Included are also timeless treasured sermons, thoughts of inspiration, moments of meditation and just all around sweet minute reflections on God's Word.

If you are somewhat as I am, you have had your moments of praise, moments of glory, moments of sadness, loneliness, disappointments and most of all moments of meditation. Maybe you have had moments when life was pushing you in on every side and there seemed to be no escape. Then suddenly you drove into the precious and priceless Word of God. In each verse you found strength for another day, another hour or just another moment.

Leaning on the promises of God, you reached into His magnanimous bag of treasures and retrieved timeless messages of hope.

Thus, is the goal of this book; to fill each heart with the glory and wisdom of God. Such wisdom can never be replaced by the pleasures of this world, which will quickly fade away.

God has made each of us special in our own way. Each unique soul touches the heart and mind of the Father. Know that you are not alone in this life's journey. Know that someone has crossed that path before you and survived whatever life threw their way. It could have been the death of a loved one, the loss of a lifetime friendship, the dissolution of a marriage or even the pain of sickness and disease. You are not alone in this fight. Your words need to be heard as well. Your pain needs to be expressed.

May our heavenly Father show you, through the pages of this book and others such as these, that, YES! Life is truly worth living and living for Jesus Christ makes it all MANIFICENT!

In the service of the King
Dr. Sharon C. Cason

CONTENTS

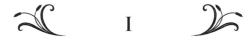

GOD WON'T LET YOU DOWN

Have you ever been set up for a letdown? Picked up to be put down? Remembered to be forgotten? Spoke up to not be heard? Or just plain old counted in only to be counted out?

So is the life story of many of the people of God but especially one saint of God in particular whose name was Jonah.

Jonah has been called 'the rebellious prophet', 'hardheaded Jonah', 'disobedient Jonah', 'stubborn Jonah', 'selfish Jonah' and yes 'wayward Jonah'.

Be it as it may, the life of Jonah is a true reflection of the lives of many a child of God today. Headed in the wrong direction, our stubborn will refuses to let us turn around. Regardless to the circumstance, we just keep reaching for the wrong stars and falling into the same old traps. Even I have found myself trying to reach a goal which I set for myself instead of pressing on to the prize which God has already set before me. Then we cry out, God why don't you hear me? God why don't you answer my prayers? Such was the case of poor old Jonah.

The first thing God said to Jonah was **"Go to Nineveh that great city and cry against it"** (Jonah 1:2) PREACH REPENTANCE! Commissioned with a task, Jonah refused to obey. Envisioning the outcome, Jonah used poor judgment and boarded a ship going in the opposite direction. Jonah knew within his heart of hearts that God would spare the city of Nineveh.

Poor old Jonah! Verse 3 says that Jonah rose up to flee unto Tarshish from the presence of the Lord. Jonah tried to willfully and purposely run from God. Jonah thought to himself, 'why should these wicked people be spared? Why should they who have defiled God's temple, killed God's prophets and rebelled against God's laws be recipients of God's grace and mercy now?'

Look at Jonah allowing bitterness and hatred to govern his life. Look at Jonah being stubborn, hardheaded and selfish. Instead of letting love, truth and righteousness reign supreme in his heart, Jonah allowed a spirit of malice to corrupt his thinking. We all must learn to let the love of God reign in our hearts. We must live a holy and righteous life, pleasing to God so that when we are called to do a task, not only will we be ready but our hearts will be ready as well.

So Jonah pays the fare, boards the ship, lies down and falls asleep (vs. 3-5). Let's add another title to the yet extensive list of names given to Jonah. Let's call him 'carefree Jonah'. Jonah was destined to flee from the presence of the Lord and God was determined not to forsake Jonah or to let Jonah down. That's the way it is for some of us. We are destined to run from the plan of God. We are destined to do things our own way. We can be stubborn, hardheaded, rebellious, selfish and carefree, just like Jonah. But God is yet determined never, ever to let us down.

God sent a storm in the sea to bring Jonah back to his senses. But old 'carefree Jonah' was fast asleep.

The men of the ship asked Jonah. What does all this mean? Call upon your God so that we will not perish. All the men of the ship tried to come to Jonah's rescue but it was Jonah's advice that they eventually heeded. Jonah said to them 'take me up and cast me forth into the sea and the sea will be calm for I know that for my sake this great tempest is upon you.'

The men tried to bring the ship to land but when they could not they took Jonah and cast him into the sea and the sea became calm just as Jonah had said. Verse 17 says *"now the Lord had prepared a great fish to swallow up Jonah and Jonah was in the belly of the fish 3 days and 3 nights.*

In the midst of the fish, Jonah cried out to God. Misery began to hold Jonah captive. Adversity surrounded Jonah on every side. Jonah had been swallowed up alive by his own selfish pride. Now faced with the possibility of sudden death and separation from God forever, he cried out in agony.

Jonah said---'***out of the belly of hell cried I. Lord you have cast me into the deep, in the midst of the sea. Thy billows and waves passed over me. The waters compassed me about, even to my soul. The deep closed around about me, the weeds wrapped about my head. I went down to the bottom of the mountains…yet thou brought up my life from corruption, O Lord my God.***'

The Lord heard Jonah's cry indeed. He spoke to the fish and it spit Jonah out on dry land. Now ready to take the Word of God seriously, Jonah arrives in Nineveh, which was a 3 day's journey, in 1 day. Jonah said to the people of Nineveh, 'in 40 days, Nineveh will be overthrown'. Jonah preached a message so powerful that the whole city repented in sackcloth and ashes.

Jonah was not surprised when the people repented. Jonah was not shocked at all when they put on sackcloth and proclaimed a fast. Jonah already knew the outcome. The people repented and God saw their works. God saw them turn from their evil ways and He repented of the evil that he had planned for Nineveh. Well, we have called him 'selfish Jonah', 'stubborn Jonah', 'carefree Jonah' and 'hardheaded Jonah'. Now let's call him angry Jonah.

Look at Jonah getting angry because he didn't get his way. Look at Jonah getting angry over a plant that sprung up over night and was struck down in one day. Look at Jonah getting angry at God for caring about the lives of sinful men, instead of being angry that over 120,000 souls would have been destroyed otherwise.

Maybe your life's story does not read quite the same way as Jonah's does. Maybe your life did not go in the same direction as Jonah's did. But truly and honestly, I believe we all can say that somewhere along the way we were drowning, sinking, being swallowed up by life's disappointments and heartaches and sometimes even our own selfish pride. The worry of life wrapped around our head until making a right decision was no longer an option. We have been afraid of failures, afraid of being alone or afraid of stepping out by faith. We have felt that Jesus was much too far away and we thought that, this time, I am going down to rise no more.

But just in the nick of time, God pulled us up. God took us by the hand and said, 'I am with you'. God picked us up out of sinking sand. And at that moment, we knew that through all the trials, through all the disturbances in life, through all that we had to face, one fact remained the same. God never let us down. God never turned his back on us. God never left us. He did not forsake us. We may fail God over and over and over again but we need to remember that God will never, ever, let us down.

Dear Heavenly Father,

I realize that you will never let me down. Not doing my times of weakness nor my moments of despair. Help me to be forever mindful of your presence even when life's waters seem to overwhelm me and the tides seem to consume me. Put a zeal in my spirit to be obedient to your will and to never ever run from your divine plan for me. In Jesus Name, I pray Amen!

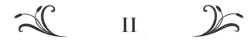

II

SHOUT UNTO THE LORD

Psalms 47:1—*"O clap your hands all ye people, shout unto God with the voice of triumph."(KJV)*

There comes a time in all of our lives when we need to release praise unto God, a praise that has been waiting to get out. A praise that tells the world, I don't care who's looking at me, I don't care who hears me, I don't care who is around me, I have to break forth with a powerful praise. I need to release a shout unto God. I need to praise God with a loud voice on high.

When you shout unto God with a voice of triumph that means that you have the victory every single day.

When you praise God, you are telling Satan that you are victorious in every area of life. It does not matter what Satan does or how he tries to pull you down, you must let him know that you are going to shout out a praise unto God. It's alright to sing and it's okay to pray but sometimes you just need to shout out a praise unto God.

The Bible tells us in Joshua 6:1-5. *"Now Jericho was shut up because of the children of Israel, none went out and none came in."* And the Lord said to Joshua, *"I have given Jericho into your hands. You shall compass the city one time for 6 days. Seven priests shall blow on 7 trumpets and on the 7ᵗʰ day you shall compass the city 7 times. And it shall come to pass, that when they make a long blast with the ram's horn, and when you hear the sound of the trumpet, all the people shall*

shout with a great shout and the wall of the city shall fall down flat…"
(KJV)

Sometimes our spirit man is shut up, no praise is going out and no praise can come in. Our spirit man is all worn down. Has your spirit man ever been worn down? Are there times when you don't want to pray? Maybe there are moments when you don't feel like reading or studying your Bible. At other times, you just put up a wall of doubt and despair.

Without our conscious consent, walls do go up and the only way to get them down is to shout them down. I'm not talking about a dance in the feet or a wave of the hand but I'm talking about a shout unto God with the praise of your lips.

Verse 16 of Joshua 6 says, ***"And it came to pass at the 7ᵗʰ time, when the priests blew with the trumpets, Joshua said unto the people-SHOUT-for the Lord hath given you the city." (KJV)***

Verse 20 says, ***"So the people shouted when the priests blew with the trumpets and it came to pass, when the people heard the sound of the trumpet and the people shouted with a great shout that the wall fell down flat, so that the people went into the city and they took the city." (KJV)***

When the people of God took the city, they found gold, brass, iron and silver in abundance.

The latter part of Psalms 132:16 declares, ***"…and the saints shall shout aloud for joy." (KJV)***

Psalms 35:27 says, ***"Let the righteous shout for joy and be glad…" (KJV)***

Psalms 32:11 says, ***"Be glad in the Lord, and rejoice ye righteous and shout for joy all ye that are upright in heart." (KJV)***

Psalms 5:11 declares, ***"Let all those that put their trust in thee rejoice, let them ever shout for joy, because thou defendeth them: let them also that love thy name be joyful in thee."*** *(KJV)*

Psalms 107:2 says, ***"let the redeemed of the Lord say so..."*** *(KJV)*

Ezra 3:10-13 reads, ***"When the builders laid the foundation of the temple of the Lord, they set the priests in their apparel with the trumpets and the Levite the sons of Asaph with cymbals, to praise the Lord...after the ordinance of David king of Israel. And they sang together by course in praising and giving thanks unto the Lord.... And all the people shouted with a great shout, when they praised the Lord. Many wept with a loud voice and many shouted aloud for joy. So that the people could not discern the noise of the shout of joy from the noise of the weeping of the people, for the people shouted with a loud shout, and the noise was heard afar off."*** *(KJV)*

I encourage you today to shout out a praise unto God with the fruit of your lips and I guarantee that your whole situation will look brighter and you will feel so much better.

Dr. Sharon C. Cason

Dear God my Father,

Look upon me today and let your glorious praises be forever in my mouth. Help me to always make time for a praise break and a hallelujah shout unto you Lord. Touch my lips and search my heart. Let me be a divine vessel of praise to you every single day. In Jesus name I pray Amen!

•

III

IT'S TIME TO SEEK THE LORD

In God's Word, we can read about King David—Israel's greatest King, Saul—Israel's first king, Solomon—Israel's wisest King, Jehoshaphat—Israel's conquering King and even Hezekiah—Israel's praying king. But now, let's read about a king named Josiah. He was a man who declared to the people that it's time to seek the Lord.

I Kings 13: 1-3 affirm---*"And behold there came a man of God out of Judah by the word of the Lord unto Bethel: and Jeroboam stood by the altar to burn incense. And he cried against the altar n the Word of the Lord, and said, O altar, altar, thus saith the Lord: Behold, a child shall be born unto the house of David, Josiah by name; and upon thee shall he offer the priests of the high places that burn incense upon thee, and men's bones shall be burnt upon thee. And he gave a sign the same day, saying, this is the sign which the Lord hath spoken; Behold, the altar shall be rent, and the ashes that are upon it shall be poured out." (KJV)*

As it was prophesied by the man of God, Josiah was indeed born. His father's name was Amon. His father did evil in the sight of the Lord. He served idols and worshipped them. He forsook the Lord and did not walk in God's way. The servants of Amon went into the king's house and killed him. The people of Judah then killed all those men who had murdered the King and they took Josiah his son and made him king instead of his father.

Josiah had a very sad and lonely childhood. At the age of 8 his father was killed and he became king. He saw violence, outrage, bloodshed and war. He had no father to show him the ways of kingship, no grandfather to teach him the true and right judgments of the Lord.

Here we see a little boy, left fatherless at the age of 8, now being made king of Israel. His mother undertook a great responsibility. It was now her job to teach her son the ways of the Lord regardless to what his father had done.

At the age of 16, taught diligently by his mother, Josiah began to seek the God of David. King Josiah turned from the ways of his father and grandfather and took his ancestor David as his role model. In all of his heart breaking moments, Josiah set his mind and will to seek the Lord. Although he was torn, battered and bruised, Josiah set his heart to seek after the true God of Israel. He did not let his past define him. He did not allow his father's brutal reign to defeat him. He turned his eyes toward the God of gods and declared to himself that 'it's time to seek the Lord'.

The Bible says that he did that which was right in the sight of the Lord and walked in all the ways of David. He did not turn from it to the left or to the right. When he was 20 years old, he began to purge Judah and Jerusalem of idolatry. He torn down the groves that his ancestors used to worship idol gods. He swept away all forms of idolatry in Judah. He completely destroyed all temples full of abominable and detestable gods made of silver, gold, wood and brass. He broke down the altars of Baalim, the carved images that were on the high places, he cut down. The molten images, he broke into pieces until they were nothing but dust. Then as prophesied, he burnt the bones of all the priests, who had sacrificed to idol gods, on the altar.

His passion drove him to get rid of everything that was a hindrance to God's people. When he was 26 years old, he began to rebuild and repair the house of God. He ordered the priests to find workers who could rebuild the house of God. He said— 'give them enough money to buy wood, stone and all manner of materials necessary to repair God's house. And they did so faithfully and without hesitation. Then King Josiah said---'set in order all the musicians, all those who are skilled with instruments and let them play skillfully before the Lord as King David had instituted'. And as they began to clear away the rubble in the temple, Hilkiah the priest found a book. It was a book of the law that God had given to Moses. Hilkiah said---'I have found the book of the Law of Moses' and they took the book and carried it to King Josiah.

The Bible declares in II Chronicles 34:19---*"And it came to pass when the King had heard the words of the law that he rent his clothes. He said to the priests—go enquire of the Lord for me and for them that are left in Israel and Judah concerning the words of the book found, for great is the wrath of the Lord that is poured out upon us because our fathers have not kept the word of the Lord, to do after all that is written in this book." (KJV)*

When they asked the Prophetess of God, Huldah, what all these words meant, she said to them, *"Thus saith the Lord, Behold, I will bring evil upon this place and upon the inhabitants thereof, even all the curses that are written in the book which they have read before the king of Judah: because they have forsaken me and have burned incense to other gods, that they might provoke me to anger with all the works of their hands; therefore, my wrath shall be poured out on this place and it shall not be quenched. And as for the king of Judah, who sent you to enquire of the Lord, so shall ye say unto him, Thus saith the Lord God of Israel concerning the words which thou hast heard; Because thine heart was tender, and thou didst humble thyself before God, when thou heardest his words against this place and against the inhabitants thereof, and didst rend thy clothes, and weep before me; I have even heard thee also, saith the Lord. Behold, I will gather thee to thy fathers and thou shalt be gathered to thy grave in peace, neither shall thine eyes see all the evil that I will bring upon the inhabitants of the same..." (II Chron. 34:24-28) (KJV)*

Then King Josiah went to the house of the Lord and all the people, great and small, gathered to hear the words of the book. Josiah the king read the words of the book of the law and he *"made a covenant before the*

Lord to walk after the Lord, and to keep his commandments, and his testimonies, and his statues, with all his heart, and with all his soul, to perform the words of the covenant which was written in this book."

King Josiah determined in his heart to keep the Passover, to put a difference between clean and unclean, holy and unholy. All the people gave willingly to the service of the Lord. They brought Passover offerings, burnt offerings and other holy things to be used in the service of God. The singers were in their place. The musicians were in their place. The Levites stood in their place and all the people kept the Passover. There was no other Passover like the one kept in the days of Josiah.

Josiah reigned 31 years in Jerusalem and Judah. All the years after they found the book of the law, the people served God with willing hearts and dedicated minds.

"…And all his days they departed not from following the Lord, the God of their fathers." (II Chron. 34:33) (KJV)

They continued to follow the ways of the Lord because Josiah was a man who sought after God like none after him had done and as the ones before him had neglected to do. His zeal and righteous acts for God are seen as a landmark of true courage and devotion to the one and only Lord of heaven and earth.

Let us seek the Lord as Josiah did. Let us come before the Lord with singing and dancing and instruments of music. Let us reach out to know the plan of God and the will of God for our lives.

"Seek ye the Lord while he may be found, call on him while he is near. Let the wicked forsake his way and the unrighteous man his thoughts and let him return unto the Lord for he will have mercy and our God will abundantly pardon." (Isaiah 55:6-7) (KJV)

"But seek ye first the kingdom of God, and his righteousness and all these things shall be added unto you." (Matthew 6:33) (KJV)

"Seek the Lord and ye shall live: ..." (Amos 5:6) (KJV)

"Seek ye the Lord, all ye meek of the earth..." (Zeph.2:3) (KJV)

"But if from thence thou shalt seek the Lord thy God, thou shalt find him, if thou seek him with all thy heart and with all thy soul" (Deut. 4:29) (KJV)

Dear Lord,

I will seek you in the morning. I will seek you in the evening. I will seek your face always. I will call upon your Holy Name through times of doubt, despair, in sickness or in health. I will make seeking your face a priority and a privilege. In the glorious name of Jesus, I make this declaration. Amen!

IV

THE ULTIMATE GIFT OF GRACE

"But God who is rich in mercy, for his great love wherewith he loved us. Even when we were dead in sins, hath quickened us together with Christ, by grace ye are saved. And hath raised us up together and made us sit together in heavenly places in Christ Jesus. That in the ages to come he might shew the exceeding riches of his grace in his kindness toward us through Christ Jesus. For by grace are ye saved through faith and that not of yourselves, it is the gift of God." (Ephesians 2:4-8) (KJV)

Sometimes people believe that the best gift is a gift given out of the kindness and generosity of the heart. Others believe that it's not the gift that matters but it's the thought that counts. Still others value the gift of money, wealth and fame above all gifts that could ever be given.

But the greatest and most valuable gift is not wrapped in a package. It is not tied up with a ribbon. The greatest gift came through the abundant love of God and the sacrificial death of Jesus Christ his Son. That gift is grace.

"Grace has been defined as---"not as a created substance of any kind, but as "the love and mercy given to us by God, because God desires us to have it, not because of anything we have done to earn it." "The condescension or benevolence shown by God toward the human race." It is understood by Christians to be a spontaneous gift from God----generous, free and totally unexpected and underserved---that takes the form of divine favor, love… and a share in the divine life of God."(Wikipedia, free encyclopedia)

Ephesians 2:4 explains that God is rich in mercy and it is because of that mercy that he loved us with a great love. It explains that even when we ourselves were dead in sins, he quickened us or made us alive.

Romans 8:11 declares-----*"But if the Spirit of him that raised up Christ from the dead dwell in you, he that raised up Christ from the dead shall also quicken your mortal bodies by His Spirit that dwelleth in you." (KJV)*

Just as God raised Jesus up so he has raised us up together with Christ. He has made us to sit in heavenly places with Christ our Savior. God our Heavenly Father did all of this in order to show the future generations how exceedingly rich his grace is.

Verse 8 of Ephesians declares: *"For by grace are ye saved through faith and that not of yourselves, it is the gift of God." (KJV)*

Grace, the unmerited favor of God is the ultimate gift.

What do we do with gifts?

Some gifts are tossed aside or tucked away in a closet. Other gifts are passed on to another person because the original recipient was not too delighted by the gift at all. Then there are gifts that are loved, cherished and adored. Such is the case with the grace of God. By grace we are saved. It is the ultimate gift.

"By grace alone, in faith in Christ's saving work and not because of any merit on our part, we are accepted by God and receive the Holy Spirit, who renews our hearts while equipping and calling us to good works" (Wikipedia, free encyclopedia)

St. John 3:16-17 declares: *"For God so loved the world that he gave his only begotten son, that whosoever believeth in him should not perish but have everlasting life. For God sent not his son into the world to condemn the world but that the world through him might be saved." (KJV)*

The life of Christ as our substitute as a living sacrifice is love and grace in action. *"Grace between God and an individual is always on the side of God for grace is the working of God Himself. Grace is the free and undeserved help that God gives us to respond to His call to become children of God…Grace is a participation in the life of God, which is poured; unearned into human beings, whom it heals of sin and sanctifies." (Wikipedia)*

St John 1:14, 16 and 17 affirms: ***"And the Word was made flesh and dwelt among us and we beheld his glory as of the only begotten of the Father, full of grace and truth. And of his fullness have we all received and grace for grace. For the law was given by Moses but grace and truth came by Jesus Christ." (KJV)***

When we speak about grace and truth, we are envisioning the kindness and love of God our Savior toward sinful men. Under grace, God gives righteousness to men, men who do not deserve His goodness and men who spurn His mercy. Even those who changed the truth of God into a lie by walking in their own self-righteousness, those he also quickened. He made us alive to Him. We were dead in our sins. We did not have any hope. We did not have a God on our side, but with His great mercy and grace, the Lord saved us. God bestowed upon us the ultimate gift when He sent His only Son to pay the penalty for sins of generations past, present and future.

Without our knowledge, we received the fullness of Christ because He gave us grace for grace, love for love, mercy for mercy and kindness for kindness.

In return He received only pain for pain, heartache for heartache, anguish for anguish and torture on top of torture. He was beaten, whipped, nailed to a cross, pierced and placed in a tomb but the richness of the grace of God raised up Christ Jesus from the dead to dwell in glory with the Father forever.

Romans 5:15 affirms: ***"but not as the offence, so also is the free gift. For through the offence of one many be dead, much more the grace of God and the gift by grace which is by one man, Jesus Christ, hath abounded unto many." (KJV)***

What is God telling us? He is saying that one man offended him. One man brought sin and death into the word and death passed upon every man because of one man's sin. Even so, now the free gift of God is offered to every man. The grace of God is poured out to us by one man as well. If one man's transgression (Adam's) caused all men to be sinners so by Jesus Christ's sacrifice can all men be made righteous by the offering of the ultimate gift of grace.

Death reigned from Adam to Moses, from Moses to the prophets, from the prophets to all men. Now, because of the free gift of grace life can reign for all men for all time and throughout eternity. Hallelujah!

But not just any kind of life; eternal life, everlasting life, life with Jesus Christ forever and ever and ever.

Romans 5:20-21 affirms: ***"the law entered that the offence might abound. But where sin abounded, grace did much more abound: that as sin hath reigned unto death, even so might grace reign through righteousness unto eternal life by Jesus Christ our Lord." (KJV)***

Yes, there was a serious offence.

Yes, there was sin involved.

And yes, that sin was great.

But it does not matter how serious the offence was or how great the sin was. What matters is that the gift of grace was greater.

We have received everything from God our Creator and we have earned nothing. He freely chose us from the beginning of time to be the recipients of His grace. Grace unites us with Christ and by being co-laborers with Him, it makes it possible for the people of God to enjoy the pleasure and privileges that the grace of God affords us. Grace saves and justifies us. Grace teaches us the plan of God but most of all, grace is sufficient for us because it is indeed the ultimate gift.

Dr. Sharon C. Cason

Dear Heavenly Father,

Thank you for giving me your grace freely. Thank you for allowing me to taste of your goodness and your love. Forgive me for taking your mercy and kindness for granted and help me to be forever grateful for your ultimate gift, the gift of grace. In Jesus' Name I pray. Amen!

MOMENTS OF MEDITATION

"Finally, brethren, whatsoever things are true, whatsoever things are honest, whatsoever things are just, whatsoever things are pure, whatsoever things are lovely, whatsoever things are of good report; if there be any virtue, and if there be any praise, think on these things." (Philippians 4,8 –KJV)

"O how love I thy law! It is my meditation all the day. I have more understanding than all my teachers: for thy testimonies are my meditation." (Psalms 119:97,99 –KJV)

"My meditation of him shall be sweet: I will be glad in the Lord." (Psalms 104:34—KJV)

"This book of the law shall not depart out of thy mouth; but thou shalt meditate therein day and night, that thou mayest observe to do according to all that is written therein: for then thou shalt make thy way prosperous, and then thou shalt have good success." (Joshua 1:8—KJV)

Oh the moments that we have wasted! Oh the hours, days, weeks and years that have been spiritually unfruitful and barren.

Somehow we allowed the cares of this world to crowd out the true meaning of life. Somehow we reached for tomorrow and grabbed a hold of yesterday;

looking back to what used to be. Somehow, we left the present to live in the future amidst a bunch of "if only", "what ifs" and "I wonder whys".

If we all were totally true to ourselves, we could honestly say that the real problem was that we failed to meditate continually on God's Word.

We need to ask ourselves:

- Was His Word my meditation early in the morning?
- Did I seek God's face before I faced each new day?
- Was a word of praise on my lips or was a complaint in my mouth?

If you answered yes to all of these questions, then you are one of those few who are about to board that chariot of fire to heaven with the prophet Elijah. But and if you answered no to some of these questions, then join the company of many baptized believers who are striving each day to please God in all that they say and do. In pleasing God, sometimes we fall short of His glory. We neglect to study His Word; our prayer life is not what it should be and most definitely, we suffer in the area of meditation.

Philippians 4:8 begins by saying: "*Finally brethren*". It is a plea to all of us to realize that after we have done all that we can do and tried to fix things our way to "finally" come to grips with the real solution to the problem. The real solution is to take our minds off of the problem and as the Apostle Paul puts it "*think on these things.*"

First of all, let's start with how to meditate on God's Word. We are not ignorant to what is written in God's Word; it's just that our minds have been programmed to dwell on other things. There are so many outside forces that crowd us from day to day, that it is almost impossible not to think about them.

There's the news!

What's happening in our world today?

Will my children be safe in school?

Who's killing whom?

Why is there so much tragedy?

There's the weather report.

Will it rain or will it snow?

Will it be hot or will it be cold?

There's our jobs, our families, our church, the fashion industry (what's in and what's out), the economy, social reform, war, peace, the homeless, the destitute, police cars speeding by, ambulance sirens going off, babies being born, hospitals full of sick people, death poll rising, stock market crashing, bombs destroying, guns being used to kill, drugs, violence, hatred, STOP!

You see! It's almost impossible not to think on these things. Therefore, we must learn how to saturate our minds with God's Word. Because we live in a world full of negativity, we must fill each gap in our lives with a positive outlook.

Despite the phrases such as "where to", "therefore" and "thus saith the Lord"; the Bible is actually the most positive book ever written.

God never condemns His people without first showing them how to avoid being in that predicament. So in order to meditate on God's Word, we must condition our minds to think as God thinks.

Well how does God think?

I know that God sees the picture as a whole, yet, I believe that God thinks in parts: simply because that is how He instructs us to think, to learn or to study His Word. In Isaiah 28:10 God instructs the prophet that he must give only portions of scripture to the people at a time.

He says:

"For precept must be upon precept…line upon line…here a little and there a little." (KJV)

He also tells us in I Peter 2:2 that *"as newborn babes'*, we must *"desire the sincere milk of the word, that ye may grow thereby:" (KJV)* For *"strong meat"* belong to those that are of full age. (Hebrews 5:14--KJV)

God never reveals His complete will for us at one time. He gradually unfolded new revelation to prophets, kings and priests, and he does the same thing for His children today.

Even though the human brain can process great quantities of information, we must learn to bring every thought into captivity or (under control) according to II Corinthians 10:5.

The Message Bible puts it this way:

"tearing down barriers erected against the truth of God, fitting every thought and emotion and impulse into the structure of life shaped by Christ."

So what is meditation? It is fitting every loose thought, emotion and impulse into the structure of life which God has shaped for you by Christ. We must learn to meditate on what God has said to us in His Word. We must learn to shape and order our lives as God would has us to.

Secondly, what are the benefits of spiritual meditation?

1. "by quieting the mind and deeply relaxing the body, the meditator experiences deep states of inner peace…and higher states of awareness." (www.Anandapaloalto.org)
2. Meditation helps us to seek greater union with God. To stand fast in one spirit with one mind" (Philippians 1:27-KJV)
3. Meditation brings success. We are to meditate on God's Word so that we can make our way prosperous and then have great success. (Joshua 1:8—KJV)

So enjoy your moments of spiritual meditation as they were your last moments on earth. Thrive on your moments of spiritual meditation with every breath that you take.

Feel your heart beating and say as King David did in Psalm 139:14---*"I will praise thee; for I am fearfully and wonderfully made: marvelous are thy works; and that my soul knoweth right well." (KJV)*

Tie up the loose ends. Fill up the gaps in your life with moments of meditation and declare:

"I will extol thee, my God, o king; and I will bless thy name forever and ever. Every day will I bless thee; and I will praise thy name for ever and ever. Great is the Lord, and greatly to be praised; and his greatness is unsearchable." (Psalms 145:1-3—KJV)

Sit back.

Relax.

Enjoy your life.

Look at the sky, the stars and the moon and say:

"O Lord our Lord, how excellent is thy name in all the earth! Who hast set thy glory above the heavens. When I consider thy heavens, the work of thy fingers, the moon and the stars, which thou hast ordained; O Lord our Lord, how excellent is thy name in all the earth!" (Psalms 8:1,3,9-KJV)

Meditate on the goodness of God and sing to yourself the words of this old hymn, "How Great Thou Art".

"Oh Lord my God, when I in awesome wonder, consider all the worlds thy hands have made. I see the stars. I hear the rolling thunder. Thy power though out the universe displayed.

Then sings my soul, my Savor, God to thee. How great Thou art. How great thou art. Then sings my soul, my Savor, God to thee. How great thou art. How great thou art.

Let your soul sing and rejoice for the greatness of the Almighty God. Allow yourself to be moved by His presence in your life. Truly God is a great God. His greatness is sometimes overwhelming and we as His children so often do not realize the vastness of His love. The next stanza reads:

When through the woods and forest glades I wander. I hear the birds sing sweetly in the trees. When I look down from lofty mountain grandeur and hear the brook and feel the gentle breeze.

Then sings my soul, my Savor, God to thee. How great thou art, how great thou art. Then sings my soul, my Savor, God to thee. How great thou art, how great thou art.

All of nature cries out to a loving, merciful and gracious God. When we look all around us and see what His hands have made, it makes us ever so grateful that one day, He decided to create mankind. Yes, my soul will sing and I will continually shout songs of praises and joy to my Father. The next stanza reads:

And when I think of God His son not sparing. Sent Him to die, I scare can take it in. That on the cross, my burden gladly bearing, he bled and died to take away my sin.

Then sings my soul, my Savor, God to thee. How great thou art, how great thou art. Then sings my soul, my Savor, God to thee. How great thou art, how great thou art.

Can you just close your eyes with me and just think of Jesus Christ dying on the cross for us? God did not hesitate to spare His only Son so that we could have a right to a home in heaven. My friends that is a lot to sing about. Then the last stanza reads:

When Christ shall come with shouts of acclamation and take me home, what joy shall fill my heart. Then shall I bow with humble adoration and then proclaim, My God How great thou art.

Then sings my soul, my Savor, God to thee. How great thou art, how great thou art. Then sings my soul, my Savor, God to thee. How great thou art, how great thou art." (www.greatchristianhymns.com)

Oh, yes, He is coming again to receive us unto Himself. Meditate on that. Think on these things and let your soul sing of His wondrous praises.

Dear Heavenly Father,

I thank you for all of your many blessings that you have given to me. Help me to appreciate your goodness and meditate on your love and mercy. Help me to make your word my meditation. Help me to fill up each gap in my life with sweet thoughts of you and your greatness. In Jesus name I pray, Amen!

VI

WORSHIPPING GOD IN SPIRIT AND IN TRUTH

"God is a Spirit: and they that worship him must worship him in spirit and in truth." (St. John 4:24—KJV)

In the Vine's Expository Dictionary, worship is defined as "devotion, honor, to render service to. Worship is not confined to praise, it may be regarded as the direct acknowledgement to God—whether by the outpouring of the heart in praise and thanksgiving or by deed done in reverence to God."

The Student Bible Dictionary defines worship as "to adore, obey, reverence, focus positive attention on. Enjoy the presence of God. Any action or attitude that expresses praise, love and appreciation for God. Worship can be expressed through obedience and the way we treat others. Worship can be private or public."

The New World Dictionary exclaims that worship is "extreme devotion or intense love or admiration of any kind, to offer prayers, attend church services, to show religious devotion to or reference for."

The term worship is sometimes applied to all of a Christian's life. It is said that everything in our lives should be an act of worship. Everything the church does as a body of believers should be considered worship, for everything we do should glorify God.

God called us, chose us and placed us into the assembly of the church so that we might worship him together, lifting up our voices as one unit, one people. Therefore, we must consider worship as a direct expression of our ultimate purpose in life which is to glorify God and fully enjoy Him forever.

When we worship, truly giving God the glory and the honor in our hearts, several things happen:

1. **We delight in God**---we experience delight in God more fully in worship than in any other activity in life. David confesses that the one thing that he will seek after above all else is – *"that I may dwell in the house of the Lord…and to inquire in his temple" Psalm 27:4—KJV)*
    King David expressed a desire just to be in the presence of the Lord above anything else that he could ever dream of. He life was one of worship, praise and devotion to God. His journey had been a difficult one. His choices had sometimes been wrong ones, yet, through all of his trials, he continued to delight in God and so should we.

2. **God delights in us**—the most amazing truth of the Scriptures is that as we, God's crowning creation, delights in Him, he in turn delights in us.
    Psalm 37:4 commissions us: *"delight thyself also in the Lord; and he shall give thee the desires of thine heart." (KJV)*

    When we love and praise God, we bring joy and delight to His heart and the greatest honor we could ever give someone is showing them how much we love them by bringing delight to their heart. When we shower our love ones with affection, life is sweeter and joy is deeper. It should be the same way with our Heavenly Father who has freely given us all things to enjoy.

3. **We draw near to God-** In the Old Covenant, the people of God could only draw near to God through burnt offerings and sacrifices. They were limited to ceremonies and rituals performed

in the flesh. Now under the New Covenant, believers have the privilege of being able to enter directly in the presence of God when they worship.

Hebrews 10:19-22 admonishes us:

"Having therefore, brethren boldness to enter into the holiest by the blood of Jesus, by a new and living way, which he hath consecrated for us, through the veil, that is to say, his flesh; and having a high priest over the house of God; let us draw near with a true heart in full assurance of faith..." (KJV)

We truly have been given a great honor. We are now able to commune with God on a day by day basis. We don't have to wait until a glory cloud appears. We do not have to experience a mountain quaking and trembling. All we have to do, to feel the presence of our Father, is enter into true and pure worship by drawing near to Him.

4. **God draws near to us**---James 4:8 declares— *"Draw nigh to God and he will draw nigh to you" (KJV)*

   This has been the pattern of God's dealing with His people throughout Biblical history. II Chronicles, chapter 5, details the account of the bringing of the Ark of Covenant into the temple built by King Solomon. The work of the temple was finished and King Solomon brought in all the things that King David, his father, had dedicated to the Lord. Solomon then assembled the elders of Israel to bring up the Ark of the Covenant to Jerusalem as well. The elders and the Levites brought up the ark and all the congregation sacrificed a multitude of sheep and oxen for the occasion. They carried the Ark and set it in the Most Holy Place in the Temple. The Levites, which were singers, along with 120 priests, which sounded the trumpets, sang and played before the Lord in King Solomon's dedicated Temple.

Verses 13 and 14 acclaim:

"It came even to pass, as the trumpeters and singers were as one, to make one sound to be heard in praising and thanking the Lord; and when they lifted up their voices with the trumpets and cymbals and instruments of music, and praised the Lord, saying; For He is good; for His mercy endureth forever; that then the house was filled with a cloud even the house of the Lord. So that the priests could not stand to minister by reason of the cloud; for the glory of the Lord had filled the house of the Lord." (KJV)

When we come together as one people, worshipping God in Spirit and in truth, God will send His glory and spirit among us.

5. **God ministers to us**---Although the primary purpose of worship is to glorify God, the Bible teaches us that in worship something else happens. We, ourselves are built up and edified. When we worship God He meets with us and directly ministers to us. He gives us strength. He grants refreshment to our spirits. He overshadows us with his love and he increases our awareness of His presence.
    Hebrew 4:16 exhorts:

    "Let us therefore come boldly unto the throne of grace, that we may obtain mercy and find grace to help in time of need. (KJV)

    II Corinthians 3:18 states:

    "And we, who with unveiled faces all reflect the Lord's glory, are being transformed into his likeness with ever increasing glory, which comes from the Lord, who is the Spirit." (NIV)

6. **The Lord's enemies flee**---When the people of Israel began to worship, God at times would fight for them against their enemies. In much the same way, when God's people offer Him worship and praise today, we may expect that the Lord will battle for us

against demonic forces that oppose the Gospel and cause them to flee as well.

II Chronicles 20:22 states:

"And when they began to sing and to praise, the Lord set ambushments against the children of Ammon, Moab and Mount Seir, which were against Judah; and they were smitten." (KJV)

Truly God is good to us and he desires our worship. But how can we enter into genuine worship? Well, let us consider the following:

- We must worship in spirit and in truth. Worship must be empowered by the Holy Spirit working within us and not by a good feeling or over expressed emotions.
- An attitude of worship begins when we see God as He is and then respond to His presence.
- Christians need to be encouraged to make right any broken relationships.
  1. Husbands need to make sure they are living considerately with their wives and honoring them in order that their prayers may not be hindered. (I Peter 3:7)
  2. The entire church is responsible to watch that no root of bitterness springs up and cause trouble in the church. (Heb.12:15)
- If we truly draw near to God in worship, we must strive for personal holiness as stated in Hebrew 12:14: *"Follow peace with all men and holiness, without which no man can see the Lord." (KJV)*
- It is important to allow enough time for worship.
  - ❖ Genuine prayer can certainly take time.
  - ❖ Solid Bible studying takes time.
  - ❖ Genuine heartfelt worship and praise will also take quite a bit of time if it is to be effective.

- Singing is especially important to worship both in the Old and New Testaments. The Psalms are loaded with exhortations to "Sing to the Lord". The following are just a few examples:
  - ❖ *"O sing unto the Lord a new song"—Psa. 98:1*
  - ❖ *"Sing unto the Lord, bless His name"—Psa. 96:2*
  - ❖ *"O come, let us sing unto the Lord."—Psa. 95:1*
  - ❖ *"It is a good thing to give thanks unto the Lord, and to sing praises unto thy name." ---Psa. 92:1*
  - ❖ *"Serve the Lord with gladness: come before His presence with singing." ---Psa. 100:2*

Dear Heavenly Father,

Forgive me falling short of your glory and help me to make sure that my praise and my worship are real, pure and true. Plant a seed of worship in my spirit that I may draw near to you and be blessed. Thank you for your presence being with me today as I stretch forth my hands in praise. This is my prayer, in Jesus Name, Amen!

VII

BLESSED AND HIGHLY FAVORED

"And in the 6th month the angel Gabriel was sent from God unto a city named Nazareth to a virgin espoused to a man whose name was Joseph, of the house of David and the virgin's name was Mary. And the angel came in unto her and said, Hail thou that art highly favored, the Lord is with thee, blessed art thou among women." (Luke 1:26-28—KJV)

The first usage of the word blessed in the Bible was in Genesis 1:22, when God blessed the sea creatures and birds telling them to be fruitful and multiply in the earth.

"A blessing, according to Merriam Webster's Collegiate Dictionary, is the act or words of one that blesses, or a thing conducive to happiness or welfare. In the Bible, there are several words that are usually translated as "blessing" or "bless". The Hebrew word most often translated "bless" is *barak*, which can mean to praise, congratulate, or salute, and is even used to mean a curse." (www.gotquestions.org)

In the New Testament, the word blessed means happy, full of life and all its goodness. "The word blessed Jesus used in the Sermon on the Mount is from the Greek word *makarios*, which means to be happy or blissful, but it also means a self-contained happiness." (www.jesus.org)

A self-contained happiness starts on the inside of an individual. It is a joy that comes only by knowing Jesus as Savor and Lord. The Beatitudes of

Matthew chapter 5 and Luke chapter 6 describe the happy state of those who find their purpose and fulfillment in God and God alone.

"Blessed are the poor in spirit: for theirs is the kingdom of heaven. Blessed are they that mourn for they shall be comforted.

Blessed are the meek: for they shall inherit the earth. Blessed are they which do hunger and thirst after righteousness for they shall be filled.

Blessed are the merciful: for they shall obtain mercy. Blessed are the pure in heart: for they shall see God.

Blessed are the peacemakers: for they shall be called the children of God.

Blessed are they which are persecuted for righteousness' sake for theirs is the kingdom of heaven.

Blessed are ye when men shall revile you and persecute you and shall say all manner of evil against you falsely, for my sake.

Rejoice and be exceedingly glad: for great is your reward in heaven: for so persecuted they the prophets which were before you." (Matthew 5:3-12—KJV)

When Jesus said all of this, He was talking about a way of life, not a catch phrase that Christians quote, but a manner of living. Regardless to what troubles you are facing or how you may feel right now, you are sincerely blessed because Jesus declared you to be. Troubles may come, as the above Scriptures state, but if happiness is a manner of life for you, you can always consider yourself blessed. But not just blessed, blessed and highly favored as well.

In verse 12 of the above scripture, Jesus said to "rejoice and be exceedingly glad". This phrase is translated several ways in different Bible versions.

- *"Be happy about it! Be very glad" (New Living Translation)*

- *"Rejoice and celebrate" (Berean Study Bible)*
- *"Rejoice and exult" (Berean Literal Bible)*
- *"Rejoice and triumph" (Aramaic Bible)*
- Be joyful and triumphant" (Weymouth New Testament)*

So you see, Jesus said all of this to us to show us that blessedness and happiness is not a catch phrase. It cannot be conjured up like some sort of potion. It cannot be earned, bought or sold. It is a state of being.

According to our reference scripture, the Angel Gabriel said to Mary— ***"Hail thou that art highly favored, the Lord is with thee, blessed art thou among women."***

Let me tell you why this virgin was blessed:

- She was blessed because she may have thought within herself---this angel is saying that I am going to conceive a child, but I don't know a man. This angel is saying, my child will be great. He will be called the Son of the Highest. My child shall reign over the house of Jacob. The angel is saying that the Holy Ghost shall come upon **ME** (just a virgin girl), the power of the Highest shall overshadow **ME** (just a shepherd's daughter). The Holy thing which shall be born of **ME**, shall be called the Son of God. She was blessed because even though she did not understand it she said---***"Behold the handmaid of the Lord; be it unto me according to thy word." (KJV)***

God is looking for a people who will obey Him. A people who will have faith in Him. A people not worried about power, position or prestige but a people concerned about love, humility and the will of God. Mary did not argue with the Angel. She did not question God. She did not say maybe tomorrow Lord or maybe when I am older, no, she said----Be it unto **ME** according to your word. Mary was willing to give her all to God. To love Him with all her heart and soul, mind and strength. That is what God requires of us today as well.

Now let me tell you why Mary was highly favored. The two words highly favored mean "to grace, to endow with special honor or to be accepted" (www.bibletools.org) Mary had the willingness and openness to live whatever life God chose to offer her and she was willing to live that life without opening her mouth to complain, to find fault or to question the will of God, the plan of God or the purpose of God. We too are to be grateful for what God has given us and we need not seek any other exit or avenue.

- Mary was highly favored because her life was clean and pure. Her mind was on the will of God and not on her own agenda.
- Mary was highly favored because she honored God with her heart and not just with her mouth.
- Mary's heart was pure. Think about the scandal, the ridicule and the ugly looks she was about to endure. She saw that she could lose all that she had worked for; her fiancé and her reputation as a virgin. She could be labeled as unfaithful. But Mary did not let these things bother her. Her heart was pure and she said figuratively ---"I'm in your hands. Be it unto me as you will.
- Mary was highly favored because she had the right spirit. She had a spirit of cooperation and submission.

If you want to be blessed and highly favored of the Lord, you must submit to the will and way of God. When you are blessed and highly favored as Mary was, you experience a fullness of the spirit of God. You realize that this is God's plan for me and come what may, I will keep a straight course and follow that plan.

The enemy wants us to think that we do not matter to God, but yes, we are blessed and highly favored. The deceiver wants us to think that God has forsaken us, but yes, we are blessed and highly favored.

We are blessed because God has declared us to be so.

We are highly favored because God has set his love upon us and given us his unmerited favor.

My friends, don't just use these words as a catch phrase. Don't just repeat void and empty words. Endeavor to be the blessed child of God that you were destined to be; and while you are pressing *"toward the mark for the prize of the high calling of God in Christ Jesus" (Philippians 3:14— KJV)* reach out and receive favor as well.

Don't be content with being blessed but be **BLESSED AND HIGHLY FAVORED OF GOD.**

Dear God my Father,

Thank you for pronouncing blessings over my life. Help me to show you how grateful I am by living a life that is pleasing to you each and every day. Show me your perfect will for my life and help me to follow your plan wherever it may take me. I know that you are in control and I trust you to the highest. I love you Lord. This is my prayer. In Jesus Name Amen!

VIII

KNOW YOUR ENEMY

"So shall they fear the name of the Lord from the west, and his glory from the rising of the sun. When the enemy shall come in like a flood, the Spirit of the Lord shall lift up a standard against him." (Isaiah 59:19—KJV)

I am not a soldier. I have never been in the army or the marine corps, but I do know that before you can defeat the enemy, you must know something about his battle strategies.

Will he attack from the rear when I am not looking, not aware of it? Yes, he will.

Will he attack me when I am weak and down and think that I don't have a friend? Yes, he will.

Will he attack me when I think that I am strong or when I am on my guard? Yes, he will.

Satan is the enemy of God's people. He has been called:

- the deceiver,
- the accuser of the brethren,
- the prince of the world
- the dragon
- the destroyer

- the prince of devils
- a roaring lion
- the adversary
- the king of death
- the ruler of darkness
- a murderer
- An angel of light
- Beelzebub
- Belial
- Lucifer
- The tempter

Satan has:

- A throne
- Doctrine
- A kingdom
- Worshippers
- Angels
- Miracles
- Armies
- Ministers

Satan does the following:

- He instigates false doctrine.
- He perverts the Word of God.
- He hinders the work of God's Servants.
- He resists the prayers of God's Servants.
- He blinds men to the truth.
- He steals the Word of God from human hearts.
- He deceives and prompts saints and sinners to transgress against the holiness of God
- He sows tares among the wheat.

This disciple of doubt thrives best when he is:

- Under-estimated
- Ignored or denied

Satan (Lucifer) was an anointed angelic being. He had pipes built within himself. He did not need to look for someone to play the organ, he was the organ. He did not have to call a praise team or a worship leader, he was the praise team all by himself. What an awesome gift to have. What a great privilege to be the worship leader in heaven. But Satan was not satisfied. Because of his beauty, he was puffed up and he tried to take over the throne of God. He tried to exalt himself above God's throne.

Isaiah 14:12-14 states:

"How art thou fallen from heaven, O Lucifer, son of the morning! How art thou cut down to the ground, which didst weaken the nations. For thou hast said in thine heart, I will ascend into heaven, I will exalt my throne above the stars of God, I will sit also upon the mount of the congregation, in the sides of the north. I will ascend above the heights of the clouds; I will be like the Most High." (KJV)

Satan's job is to do all that he can do to block or stop the plan of God from being fulfilled. He knows that in the end, we win and he loses. He will be cast into a lake of fire and into a bottomless pit.

If we are to have victory over Satan we must know his weakness' and strengths.

- Satan's strengths lie in our weakness. He does not care if we preach all day. He could care less if we sing ourselves silly, as long as we do not mean it from our heart. His strength comes when we straddle the fence, do not live holy and claim to be a child of God when we are not. *"Straddling the fence in life means to support both sides of an issue. We don't want to commit to either side because we are afraid of making a mistake or possibly because we want what both sides have to offer." (WordPress.com)*. The true children of God are those who are more than willing to make a full and total commitment to the will of God.

- Satan's greatest weakness is the blood of Jesus. He cannot tolerate the blood. It is the blood that saves, heals, delivers and sets the captives free, therefore we must learn how to plead the blood of Jesus against him. *"Pleading the blood simply means applying the blood to our life and circumstances just like the Israelites applied it to their door posts and were protected from the destroyer (Exodus 12). Pleading the blood is simply the taking hold of the authority and power available to us by the death and resurrection of Jesus." (www.wordlibrary.co.uk)*

- Satan cannot stand to be resisted. That is why, we must resist him at all costs. *"The phrase "resist the devil" is found in James 4:7 where the apostle James exhorts believers to resist the devil in order to cause him to flee or "run away" from us. To resist means to withstand, strive against, or oppose in some manner…Using the Scriptures to expose Satan lies and temptations is the most effective way to strive against and defeat him…Resisting the devil must be accompanied by submitting to God. A disobedient or non-submissive believer will not see victory." (www.gotquestions.org)*

- He cannot tolerate the prayers of the saints. *"Since we belong to God, Satan intends to frustrate, afflict, or suppress us and allow us no foothold. This is his aim, although his aim may not be achieved because we may approach the throne of grace by the precious blood of the Lord Jesus, asking for God's protection and care. As God hears our prayer, Satan's plan is definitely defeated." (Prayer that resists Satan- Watchman Nee)*

- He cannot tolerate the praises of the saints. We must remember that Satan was the worship leader in heaven. *"Satan hates you because you have stolen his job, and you're better at it than he was… the worship he brought to God was the most beautiful thing in all the cosmos, but he lost his way and when he lost his way he lost his job." (www.charismanews.com)*

- Now, the children of God are committed to praise God. Our praise is a reflection of God's glory. His love for us is a love like no other. The peace of God is a peace that does not come from outside sources. The joy that the Lord gives us is one that mends hearts and heals broken wounds. In remembering all of this, we are exhorted to praise God with every fiber of our being. Hallelujah!

Satan disguises himself and makes us think that he is an angel of light. You may think that your sister is your enemy. Maybe the preacher is the enemy. Maybe it's your spouse, your children or even your parents. No, my friends, Satan would have us to think that this is so but we must see him for who he is, the real enemy.

Dear Heavenly Father,

Open our eyes so that we may see the real enemy, which is Satan. Do not allow the enemy to bind us, blind us or destroy us but give us more power of your Holy Spirit that we may be aware of his tactics and recognize him, fight against him and resist him at all costs. In the precious name of Jesus, we pray, Amen!

IX

A BED OF ROSES NEVER LOSES IT'S THORNS

"And lest I should be exalted above measure through the abundance of the revelations, there was given to me <u>a thorn in the flesh,</u> the messenger of Satan to buffet me, lest I should be exalted above measure".

"And he said unto me, my grace is sufficient for thee: for my strength is made perfect in weakness. Most gladly therefore will I rather glory in my infirmities, that the <u>power of Christ may rest upon me</u>." (II Corinthians 12:7,9—KJV)

I love roses! Most women do! We love roses for their beauty, smell and the message behind them. Not only do we love roses, but we love receiving bouquets of roses, regardless to the occasion. We love Roses that say "I love you". We love roses that say "I'm sorry" or that just say "I was thinking about you".

"The rose is considered a symbol of balance. The beauty of this flower expresses promise, hope and new beginnings. It is contrasted by thorns symbolizing defense, loss and thoughtlessness." (undergroundinkcny.com)

The rose is the most enduring symbol of love and appreciation that has outlasted the test of time. It is deeply admired and favored among all other flowers. Each rose color has its own special significance to us who appreciate the beauty of the sure and steadfast promises of God our Father.

The red rose has been *"associated with beauty and perfection, red roses are a time-honored way to say "I love you". (www.proflowers.com)*

"A classic symbol of grace and elegance, the pink rose is often given as a token of admiration and appreciation." (www.proflowers.com) The bright and beautiful pink roses say— "I appreciate you" and the love, patience and kindness that we have shared.

"White roses are traditionally associated with marriages and new beginnings, but their quiet beauty has also made them a gesture or remembrance. The white rose says— "I'm thinking of you" It stands for marriage, spirituality and a new start." (www.proflowers.com)

"With their blazing energy, orange roses are the wild child of the rose family. Whatever feelings you might be bubbling over with---enthusiasm, passion, gratitude—oranges roses will get the message across." (www.proflowers.com)

"When it comes to sending a joyful message, yellow roses are your best friend. Yellow roses are a traditional symbol of friendship. Yellow roses have a tendency to light up the room, saying "thanks', "get well", "congratulations" or just "thanks for being you". (www.proflowers.com)

The rose is considered to be the most "perfect" of all flowers. It is always lavished upon, conversed about, cherished, used in poetry to express love and remains to be a symbol of beauty and admiration.

The rose expresses promise, hope and love.

The thorns express defense, loss and an uncaring spirit.

Taken together as one unit and one entity, the rose is really a symbol of love, joy and peace but at the same time bares thorns, which stand on guard against loss and defends itself against an unyielding individual who would only trifle underfoot the true characteristics of their intended loved one.

If you have ever examined a rose, you would have noticed that each rose petal is full of vibrant color and energy. The rose petals are soft and exuberant to the touch. When you see a multi-colored rose you are experiencing a perfect blend of extravagant richness.

The rose says "I love you" and at the same time says "I know you". It says "I am willing to suffer loss, pain and hurt because of you", yet, "I still love you as you are." That is what Jesus Christ said to us.

"Jesus is perfect love just as the rose is the most perfect of all flowers in its looks, beauty and smell" …Nowhere in the New Testament is Jesus actually referred to as the Rose of Sharon. However, He is symbolically referred to as the Rose of Sharon by many…Sharon is a plain and 'back at the time of Solomon' it was considered a wild, fertile plain that had many beautiful flowers in it. Sharon was supposed to have been known for its beauty and majesty" (www. bible-knowledge.com)

Song of Solomon 2:1 states:"

I *am the Rose of Sharon, the lily of the valley. (KJV)*

Sharon was a valley where the best roses grew. Many have used this phrase as a characteristic of Jesus Christ.

"By using the rose flower as a visual symbolism of Jesus' love for us, we can better see and appreciate what God is trying to tell us in the personal love relationship that he wants to establish with each and every one of us…He wants all of us to realize how special His love is for us, and that He wants more than anything else to be able to enter into this personal love relationship with each one of us." (www.bible-knowledge.com)

Let's take a retrospective look at the life of the Apostle Paul. He was a man who could have, indeed, gloried in his accomplishments, but he would not. Apostle Paul taught the Gospel of Christ to the first century world. Before becoming the great missionary evangelist, Paul was known as Saul the persecutor of the Christian church. He is "often considered to be the second most important person in the history of Christianity"; Jesus Christ being the first. "His …letters…had enormous influence on subsequent

Christianity and secured his place as one of the greatest religious leaders of all time." (www.Britannica.com)

Paul tells how "he was caught up into paradise and heard unspeakable words, which is not lawful for a man to utter." (II Cor. 12:4—KJV) He also said in verse 1 of the same chapter of Corinthians that he was "come to visions". Visions of heaven, visions of the risen Christ and even visions that were yet to be fulfilled. In verse 12, he said that the signs of a true apostle were given to him and shown to the other apostles.

So you see, he had every reason to glory but he said "yet of myself, I will not glory, but in mine infirmities." (verse 5) Verse 7 tells why the Apostle Paul did not glory in his accomplishments. It explains to us that to keep Paul humble and highly anointed, there was given to him "a thorn in the flesh". The messenger of Satan was sent to buffet him, to test him and to disturb him.

The Apostle Paul was handed a bed of roses; abundant revelations were given to him. Oh! how privileged he must have felt to be able to commune with the Father continuously.

Figuratively, he was surrounded by a bed of roses. Roses that represented strength and beauty, love and joy, hope and appreciation. Roses of all colors and sizes. Roses in abundance. Roses of all types of representations.

Nevertheless, he was constantly being pricked by the thorns of life that accompanied the roses. He was torn between serving God and suffering persecution. He was stoned, beaten, imprisoned and finally, he gave his life for the cause of Christ. His life was one of total commitment. It came with its advantages but also its miseries.

Yes! The roses had their thorns and each rose in his life brought its own overwhelming beauty, yet, along with the rose came the gruesomeness of life's true colors.

God had given life in the Garden of Eden, abundant life, eternal life and life without pain but sin entered in and upset life's natural balance. Now, all of us have to accept life with thorns.

In the book of Matthew, chapter13, Jesus gave us the parable of the sower. He declared:

"Behold, a sower went forth to sow. And when he sowed, some seeds fell by the way side and the fowls came and devoured them up: Some fell upon stony places, where they had not much earth and forewith they sprung up, because they had no deepness of earth, and when the sun was up, they were scorched, and because they had no root, they withered away. And some fell among thorns and the thorns sprung up and choked them: But others fell into good ground and brought forth fruit, some an hundredfold, some sixtyfold and some thirtyfold." (KJV)

Here, we see, that the seeds which were sown were devoured, scorched by the sun, choked by thorns and others brought forth fruit.

Let us consider, above the others, the thorns. The thorns choked the seed, so much so, that it made it impossible for them to grow.

The thorns sprang up along with the seed. The natural beauty of the seeds did not appear without the natural defense mechanism, which were the thorns. Each of us has a built in defense mechanism. We can choose to put up a wall to keep out all negativity or we can allow the positive and negative to co-exist, as the rose does.

The thorns do exist, that is a true fact of life, but those thorns do not have to choke up. We can try to separate the joy from the sadness. We can focus so much on the rain that we miss the rainbow that's coming after the storm or we can live each day in anticipation and expectation.

Jesus spoke another parable in Matthew 13:24-30. He declared:

"the kingdom of heaven is likened unto a man which sowed good seed in his field. But while he slept, his enemy came and sowed tares

among the wheat and went his way. But when the blade sprung up, and brought forth fruit, then appeared the tares also. So the servants of the house holder came and said unto him, Sir, didst not thou sow good seed in thy field? From whence then hath it tares?

He said unto them, an enemy hath done this. The servants said unto him, wilt thou that we go and gather them up? But he said, Nay, lest while ye gather up the tares, ye root up also the wheat with them. Let both grow together until the harvest and at the time of the harvest, I will say to the reapers, gather ye together first the tares and bind them in bundles to burn them but gather the wheat into my barn." (KJV)

Jesus was explaining to us through this parable that we cannot separate the pain in life from the joys in life. We must, as Jesus stated, allow them both to "grow together" and in the end, He will do the separating.

He promised us in Revelation 21:4:

"And God shall wipe away all tears from their eyes; and there shall be no more death, neither sorrow, nor crying, neither shall there be any more pain: for the former things are passed away." (KJV)

And if I may add, no more thorns.

That brings us back to our thought for today: a bed of roses never loses its thorns. We cannot expect to have a bed of roses without the thorns. We cannot live free from agony without first experiencing pain; and we will never, in this life, be able to open our eyes to a bright new sunny day without first being engulfed by the darkness that night brings.

So remember, my friends, a bed of roses never loses its thorns. Be it a thorn in the flesh, as Apostle Paul experienced. Be it a thorn of doubt, a thorn of sickness, a thorn of a broken marriage or a thorn of financial difficulties.

Though these thorns may prick or bruise you, be assured that each trial in your life will eventually come to an end. The final outcome, however, lies in your hands. You can allow the thorns in life to defeat you, to choke you or to buffet you or you can use each thorn as a stepping stone to victory.

Dear Heavenly Father,

Teach me how to depend on you and not on my own capabilities. Show me the thorns in life and do not allow them to control and conquer me. I thank you for each new day and each new experience but especially for the thorns in life that are making me stronger. Let me appreciate the beauty of your world which surrounds me and yet still be aware of the dark clouds that may hover over me. In Jesus Name I pray, Amen!

This section is dedicated to my sister, Vivian T. Parker, who reminded me that a bed of roses never loses its thorns and to my husband and children who despite being pricked by the thorns, have always seen me as their own personal "Rose of Sharon".

X

GOD IS ONLY ONE PRAYER AWAY

"Offer unto God thanksgiving and pay thy vows unto the Most High, and call upon me in the day of trouble, I will deliver thee and thou shalt glorify me." (Psalms 50:14,15—KJV)

What is prayer?

Prayer is the communing of one being to another being higher than himself. Some of us call that being God. Some call Him "Elohim" of "Jehovah". Others call Him "Yahweh" or "Heavenly Father" and some even call Him, "the man upstairs".

Regardless to what He is called, prayer, is a prevailing. It is crying out to God out of the depths of our soul. Prayer is the link in the chain that connects us to the Father.

The Scriptures admonishes us to call on God in the day of trouble and God promises that He will deliver us. He promises to give us our heart's desire and He has promised to answer our prayers. Now, that answer may not be what we think it should be but God alone knows exactly what we need, even before we ask Him.

When it seems as if God is not answering your prayer, it does not mean that He does not hear your prayer.

There are several reasons why some prayers remain unanswered:

1. The presence of sin in our lives disrupts the flow of God's blessings and answers to prayers.

   David declared in Psalm 66:18:

   "If I regard iniquity in my heart, the Lord will not hear me." (KJV)

   If you are seeking an answer from God concerning life's struggles, you must make sure that your spiritual life is lining up with God's word. According to the Apostle John, answers to prayers come when we seek Him and keep His Word.

   I John 3:22 affirms:

   "And whatever we ask we receive from Him, because we keep His commandments and do those things that are pleasing to Him." (KJV)

2. Sometimes unanswered prayers are a result of wrong motives and desires in prayer.

   James 4:3 states:

   "You ask and do not receive, because you ask amiss, that you may consume it in your lusts." (KJV)

3. I John 5:14 declares:

   "And this is the confidence that we have in him, that, if we ask anything according to His will, He heareth us." (KJV)

   This means that some prayers go unanswered, simply, because it is not in God's will.

4. The greatest reason, probably, why some prayers are left unanswered is because many people just give up and stop praying and believing.

   Galatians 6:9 admonishes us:

   "Be not weary in well doing for in due season we will reap if we faint not." (KJV)

   God has a due season for us and He will bring the answer to pass. We should never stop believing, regardless to how long it takes.

   I John 5:15 assures us:

   "And if we know that he hear us, whatsoever we ask, we know that we have the petitions that we desired of him." (KJV)

5. And sometimes prayers are unanswered because we are too far away from God. In order for God to hear and answer your cry, you must get closer to Him and the only way to get closer to God is through prayer.

Luke 18:1 declares:

"And Jesus spoke a parable unto the people that men ought to always pray and not to faint." (KJV)

Prayer draws us nearer and nearer to the throne of God. It does not have to be a long prayer but it should be a sincere and heartfelt prayer that reaches the heart and mind of the Father. In praying, we must exhibit confidence and assurance that God will answer us regardless to how long it takes.

James 5:13-16 declare: *"Is any among you afflicted? Let him pray. Is any merry? Let him sing psalms. Is any sick among you? Let him call for the elders of the church; and let them pray over him, anointing him with oil in the name of the Lord.*

And the prayer of faith shall save the sick and the Lord shall raise him up; and if he have committed sins, they shall be forgiven him. Confess your faults one to another, and pray one for another, that ye may be healed. The effectual fervent prayer of a righteous man availeth much." (KJV)

To be effective, prayer must be passionate. One must truly believe in what he or she is praying for and about. Prayer can and does make a big difference in this world but we must understand that it takes an effort and sacrifice to pray effectively.

Let me share with you, seven steps to effective prayer:

1. **Take the time to pray**
   Give God some of your time. Time is precious and it is valuable. It can never be replaced. Nor can you ever relive this life. So you must, I must, we must, make the best of the time that we have by

giving back to God, some of the time he has so freely given to us. There is a song that I used to love so dear, and it is entitled "Time in a Bottle" by Jim Croce. The words still ring so true and clear. It says: "If I could save time in a bottle, the first thing that I'd like to do, is save every day till eternity passes away, just to spend them with you. If I could make days last forever, if words could make wishes come true. I'd save every day like a treasure and then, again, I would spend them with you. But there never seems to be enough time to do the things you want to do, once you find them, I've looked around enough to know that you're the one I want to go through time with." (www.azlyrics.com)

Now, who, he was referring to is not clear, but if we allow God to come into the equation and save time to spend with Him, every empty place in our lives would be filled. Every dry place would be overflowing with springs of living water and every sincere desire and need would be met.

2. **Find a good location to pray**

    Matthew 5:5-7 declares:

    "And when thou prayest, thou shalt not be as the hypocrites are: for they love to pray standing in the synagogues and in the corners of the streets, that they may be seen of men. Verily I say unto you, they have their reward.

    But thou, when thou prayest, enter into thy closet, and when thou hast shut the door, pray to thy Father which is in secret; and thy Father which seeth in secret shall reward thee openly. But when ye pray, use not vain repetitions, as the heathen do: for they think that they shall be heard for their much speaking." *(KJV)*

    Here, Jesus is teaching a very important lesson on prayer. He makes several key points:

    - Do not be as the hypocrites are. They stand in the streets and on the corner to be seen of men. There is a time and proper place for prayer. We do not pray to show off or for recognition. We pray for answers.

- Jesus says, pray in secret and when your Heavenly Father sees that you are committed to prayer, He will answer you and reward you openly.

- Do not use vain repetitions. Do not speak a lot of empty words and do not make a lot of promises in prayer, because our Heavenly Father knows what we need even before we ask Him.

3. **Get into a prayer position.**

   It could be standing, sitting or kneeling. You can have your hands raised, your head bowed or your head raised to heaven. You may even be lying on your face before the Lord.

   In the insect kingdom, there is a preying mantis (preying). This mantis seems to be in a position of prayer all the time. His hands are always together as if he is praying, but actually he is in a position to attack. Whatever comes along for dinner, be it a spider, a fly or a mosquito, he attacks it in a split second that it's almost impossible to catch it on camera.

   Just like that preying mantis, we too have to constantly be in a position for prayer, so that whatever problem or situation comes along, we are ready to attack it with prayer.

4. **Prepare for prayer**

   Anoint yourself with the oil of gladness. Put your cell phone on silent. Turn off the television. Put on some nice soft music or sing and make melody in your heart to the Lord. When we bring our petitions before God, we must be in the right attitude for prayer.

5. **Begin your prayer by calling on the name of the Lord**

   Psalm 100:4 declares:

   "Enter into His gates with thanksgiving and into His courts with praise: be thankful unto Him and bless His name." (KJV)

   When you enter into God's presence, be thankful. Thank Him for what He has already done before you ask Him to do anything else.

6. **Make your requests known**

   Philippians 4:6 declares: ***"Be careful for nothing, but in everything by prayer and supplication with thanksgiving, let your requests be made known unto God." (KJV)***

7. **End your prayer**

When you end your prayer, it is final. When you say Amen! you say it is so and you expect the answer to come by faith. When you say in Jesus' name, you say by faith that He can do it. You take a step forth in faith; a step toward God and not away from God. When you say, in the name of the Father, Son and Holy Spirit, you are turning the situation over to God. You are taking it out of your hands and putting it in God's hands. You are releasing it to God.

Remember my friends, that the victory is yours to have if you will receive it. Complete and total victory awaits us in the presence of the Lord and when we have victory, we are well able to handle whatever life throws our way. For God, our Heavenly Father, our Yahweh, our Elohim, Our El Shaddai, is only one prayer away.

Dear Heavenly Father,

We give you thanks and praise today for being available. Thank you for hearing and answering our prayers as we approach your throne. Give us the peace and victory we need to overcome the enemy. Teach us how to be bold soldiers for you in this fight and never allow us to waver, stumble or fall from grace. Help us to continue to seek you in all areas of our lives. In Jesus' Name we pray. Amen!

XI

HOW CAN WE KNOW GOD?

"But what things were gain to me, those I counted loss for Christ. Yea doubtless, and I count all things but loss for the excellency of the knowledge of Christ Jesus my Lord: for whom I have suffered the loss of all things, and do count them but dung, that I may win Christ, and be found in Him, not having mine own righteousness, which is of the law, but that which is through faith of Christ, the righteousness which is of God by faith: That I may know Him and the power of his resurrection and the fellowship of His sufferings, being made conformable unto His death." (Philippians 3:7-10-KJV)

We spend our lives engrossed in multitudes of books, commentaries and even opinions of others; searching out countless ways in which we may know God. Yet, we may never come to the full realization of who God is and why Jesus Christ entered into this sinful world to save us. Theologians, Christian workers, prophets and teachers have searched diligently to gain knowledge about God, without truly knowing God themselves.

The knowledge to talk about God and the propensity to discuss Christian themes is not the same thing as knowing God. To know ourselves is to know God for we were created in the image and likeness of God.

God spoke to the Prophet Isaiah saying;

"Hear, O heavens, and give ear, O earth: for the Lord hath spoken, I have nourished and brought up children and they have rebelled against

me. The ox knoweth his owner and the ass his master's crib: but Israel doth not know, my people doth not consider." (Isaiah 1:2-3—KJV)

We have not really considered how great God is, nor have we taken into account the goodness of God. Many of us have yet to develop that oneness with God that comes from a personal relationship with Jesus Christ. For to know God is to love Him and to love Him is to serve Him.

But how can we really know God? We do not simply want to know facts about Him or actions that he does. We want to be assured that it is God Himself that we know.

Let me share with you several ways in which we can know God:

1. **We can know God through His Word.**
   In the Scriptures God revealed several facts about Himself to His people.
   - *"I am God, and there is none else; I am God, and there is none like me." (Isa. 46:9—KJV)*
   - *"I the Lord thy God am a jealous God" (Exo. 20:5-KJV)*
   - *"For I am the Lord, I change not..." (Mal. 3:6-KJV)*
   - *"God is not a man, that he should lie; neither the son of man, that he should repent'..."(Num. 23:19-KJV)*
   - *"For our God is a consuming fire." (Heb. 12:29-KJV)*
   - *"God is a Spirit."—(John 4:24—KJV)*
   - *"God is love."---(I John 4:8---KJV)*

   We can know God through His word, because God is who He says He is. All the Scriptures are God's words. We can choose to believe or disbelieve. To know the very words of God is to have confidence in our hearts that we are receiving directly from the mouth of God, who cannot lie. The Bible is the infallible work of God. Many books have been written but the Bible outsells them all. Though refuted, rebutted and rebelled against, the Bible stands as the ultimate standard of truth. Therefore, to know what God says in His word "the Bible' is to know God.

2. **It is possible to know God through observing the world around us.**

King David exclaimed in Psalms 19:1-2:

"The heavens declare the glory of God; and the firmament sheweth his handiwork. Day after day uttereth speech and night unto night sheweth knowledge." (KJV)

When we look at the sky, we see evidence of the power, wisdom and beauty of God. These evidences of God's love, mercy and joy are all around us in creation and can be clearly seen. Even those who live by their own wickedness, cannot avoid the proofs of God's existence.

Romans 1:19-21 states:

"Because that which may be known of God is manifest in them; for God hath showed it unto them. For the invisible things of him from the creation of the world are clearly seen, being understood by the things that are made, even his eternal power and God-head: so that they are without excuse: Because that, when they knew God, they glorified him not as God, neither were thankful; but became vain in their imaginations and their foolish heart was darkened." (KJV)

All of creation gives evidence that God created all things. Many may deny this fact but it is only because their hearts and minds have been blinded to the truth.

3. **We can also know God through the observation of ourselves.**

Psalms 139:14 declares:

"I will praise thee, for I am fearfully and wonderfully made..." (KJV)

Genesis 1:27 states:

"So God created man in his own image, in the image of God created he him, male and female created he them." (KJV)

Genesis 2:21-22 further state:

"And the Lord caused a deep sleep to fall upon Adam and he slept: and he took one of his ribs and closed up the flesh instead thereof and the rib which the Lord God had taken from man, made he a woman and brought her unto the man." (KJV)

All of these Scripture references show a skilled physician at work; molding, making, operating and creating a masterpiece. He created a work of art which could not have come from billions of years of evolution, but only from the hands of an all-loving, and all-wise Creator.

We can hear music playing, birds singing and children laughing. We can see the colors of a rainbow, the redness of a rose and the brightness of white in the snow. All of these things declare to us that God is a God of love and a God of pleasure; for He allows us to experience happiness and joy even through pain and sorrow.

Jesus declared in Luke 12:7:
"But even the very hairs of your head are all numbered..." (KJV)
Why would God take the time to number the hairs on our head? Why would God cause every organism, every cell, every nerve, muscle and vessel in the body to work together in an orderly fashion?

Why? Because our God is truly amazing and Yes! we are fearfully and wonderfully made.

4. **We can know God through praise and worship.**
   Through the praise and worship of God, we fellowship with God. Praise and worship is the key to knowing God, for it causes us to know God, Himself, and not just mere facts about Him.
   God spoke to the prophet Jeremiah saying:
   "Thus saith the Lord, let not the wise man glory in his wisdom, neither let the mighty man glory in his might, let not the rich man glory in his riches: But let him that glorieth glory in this, that he understandeth and knoweth me, that I am the Lord which exercise loving-kindness, judgment and righteousness

in the earth: for in these things I delight, saith the Lord."
(Jeremiah 9:23-24—KJV)

A relationship with God is very essential to knowing God, Himself and it is through worship and praise of God that we develop this type of relationship. We are connected to God as we commune with Him in prayer. We interact with God as we show Him, through our praises, how thankful and grateful we really are to Him. We relate to God when we worship Him for who He is.

5. **Finally, to know the love of God is to know God.**
   Romans 5:8 states:
   "but God commendeth his love toward us in that while we were yet sinners, Christ died for us." (KJV)

To know God's love is to experience heaven on earth. God's love finds expression in everything that He says and does. We, the children of God, have the assurance that we are loved by our Heavenly Father. Everything that happens to us expresses God's great love for us, even when we cannot see His purpose and plan for our lives.

God's love finds its fulfillment in the manifestation of Christ's provision for the salvation of sinful men. To know the love of God and how much Christ sacrificed for us and to what measure God went to save us, is truly to know God.

The knowledge of God can be summed up with exerts from a children's book written by Virginia L. Knoll—entitled <u>I wanted to know all about God</u>:

"I wanted to know all about God, so I went out looking for Him in signs of His creation.
I wondered what God does in the morning, then I smelled the dew on the grass at dawn.
I wondered if God is gentle, and a butterfly floated on the air in front of me.

I wondered if God is strong and the ocean roared in my ears.

We learn about a loving and awesome God through the things that we see around us. The dew on the grass, a bright and beautiful butterfly, painted by the hands of God or the sound of the ocean.

I wondered how God's reflection looks when he smiles
and the snow glittered in the sun.
I wanted to know if God likes music,
then I heard a pond on a summer night.
I wanted to know what colors God likes,
then I met several children of other races.
I wondered if God's people have faith in each other
and my friend trusted me with a secret.

We understand the wonders of God by observing the pureness of snow, the colors of creation and the friends that we share.

I wondered if God is caring and the new boy shared his crayons with me.
I wondered what God's love feels like
and Grandma put her arms around me and gave me a hug.
I wanted to know where God likes to visit and I felt someone knocking at my heart.
Now when I go out looking for God, I know exactly where to find Him."

Truly, knowing God is a privilege and a pleasure. If there is anyone who does not know God, it's never too late to seek Him and find Him.

Dr. Sharon C. Cason

Dear Heavenly Father,

My desire is to know you more and more each day. Give me the wisdom and courage to seek after you with all of my heart. Help me to know you as you know me. I praise you because you have opened my eyes to see how truly wonderful you are. In Jesus Name I pray. Amen!

•

XII

THE LORD NEEDS YOU

"And when he had thus spoken, he went before ascending up to Jerusalem. And it came to pass, when he was come nigh to Bethphage and Bethany at the mount called the Mount of Olives, he sent two of his disciples. Saying go ye into the village over against you in the which at your entering ye shall find a colt tied, whereon yet never man sat, loose him and bring him hither. And if any man ask you why do you loose him? Thus shall ye say unto him, Because the Lord hath need of him." (Luke 19:28-31—KJV)

The Bible says that Jesus instructed two of his disciples to go into the village and when they entered the village, they would find a colt tied up. Jesus said to "loose him and bring him hither" (to me) And if any man asks them why they were loosing the colt, they were to say that the Lord has need of it.

The disciples were completely obedient and as they went, they found the colt just as Jesus had said. When they began to loose the colt, the owner said to them: **"why are you untying the colt?" (NIV)**, And the disciples said to him: **"the Lord needs it." (NIV)**

My friends, God needs you. When the disciples were told to go, they hastened and went to do what Jesus had instructed them to do. When they brought the colt to Jesus, they spread their garments on the colt and sat Jesus on it. But they did not stop there; as they went through the streets of Jerusalem, they took theirs clothes and spread them in the way. Others took down palm branches and placed them in the way. They were saying, Blessed be the King that cometh in the name of the Lord.

Some of them said:

"Hosanna to the son of David: Blessed is he that cometh in the name of the Lord: Hosanna in the highest." (Matthew 21:9—KJV)

They recognized Jesus for who He was. King of kings and Lord of lords. Jesus did not need the disciples to go and get the colt. He could have gotten the colt himself, but for the sake of the Kingdom, he instructed his disciples to do it. Here Jesus taught them a very valuable lesson, that is "if it is to be, it's up to me".

It is up to you and I to fulfill the mission that Jesus gave to us. Without us, the kingdom of God cannot stand. Jesus needs men and women, boys and girls, the rich and the poor. He needs people everywhere to carry out the work that he started; the work of saving souls and building up the church of God, which He purchased with His own blood.

When Christ came into Jerusalem, God put it into the hearts of the whole multitude, not just the disciples, to praise Him. That lets us know today, that God needs all of us, not just a few of us. We can win souls for Christ if we allow him to use us, all of us. We can do a mighty work for God if we yield ourselves to His will.

We are very important to God. We have gifts and talents that He has placed within us. There is no one like you or I, God made us special and unique.

Sometimes we may feel as if there is nothing that we can do for God; but God has invested His time and love into us, He made us who we are. We are His pride and joy. We are His crowning creation. Your birth was not an accident. You were meant to be here. It does not matter if your life is all messed up right now; because God can fix it up. God can clean you up because he needs you. God is willing to wait until you are ready to give your all to Him.

Maybe you are frustrated, confused, disappointed or even have been hurt and bruised by the cares of this life; but it does not matter what happened in the past, God wants to give you a glorious future.

You are destined for greatness. There is a spirit that God has put inside of you and with that spirit you connect to God. So when times get hard, as they will, and it seems as though you cannot make it, just keep telling yourself----"I am connecting with God" --- "God has given me favor" ---"I cannot stop now" ---"the Lord needs me".

If you see the tide coming into the shore, don't stay there and get swept away by the waters and the waves; move out in faith. Don't give up because the waters look rough; move out in faith expecting God to do great things.

You may have been through a thousand disappointments. You may have been knocked down a thousand times; but don't stay down, get back up. Sometimes you just need a push in the right direction. God knows the dreams that He put within you. He knows exactly where you are in life. He even knows the secrets and intents of your heart.

In Jeremiah 29:11, God said:

"For I know the thoughts that I think toward you saith the Lord. Thoughts of peace and not of evil, to give you an expected end. Then shall ye call upon me and ye shall go and pray and I will hearken unto you unto you. And ye shall seek me and find me, when ye shall search for me with all your heart." (KJV)

God is not going to give up on you. He will not disqualify you, because He needs you.

- God needs your faith
  In order for God to work on your behalf, it is necessary that you have faith. Faith moves mountains. It's your faith that works wonders and it is your faith that calls forth deliverance.
- God needs your tongue

He needs your tongue to speak the right words so that He can get things moving for you. He needs you to speak words of faith and not doubt; to speak life into those dry bones. He needs you to call those things that are not, as though they were. You must call in victory and blessings. You must call in salvation and favor. God is trying to pull you into your divine destiny but you must stop pulling away from Him.

- God needs your worship

  When you worship the Lord, you release favor in your life. You release healing for your body and you release the power of the Holy Spirit into your life.

  Psalms 95: 1-3,6:

  "O come, let us sing unto the Lord: let us make a joyful noise to the rock of our salvation. Let us come before his presence with thanksgiving, and make a joyful noise unto him with psalms. For the Lord is a great God, and a great King above all gods...O come, let us worship and bow down; let us kneel before the Lord our maker." (KJV)

- God needs your praise

  Psalms 150 declares:

  "Praise ye the Lord. Praise God in His sanctuary, praise Him in the firmament of His power, praise Him for His mighty acts, praise Him according to His excellent greatness, praise Him with the sound of the trumpet and dance: praise him with stringed instruments and organs. Praise him upon the loud cymbals: praise him upon the high sounding cymbals. Let everything that hath breath praise the Lord. Praise ye the Lord." (KJV)

- Most of all, God needs your hands and feet

  God needs all of us to go into the hedges and highways. He needs us to go into the vineyards and work so that His house will be full.

My friends, God really needs you.

Dear Heavenly Father,

Forgive me for not conforming to your will and help me to make myself available for your service. Help me to realize what you have invested in me that I may seek your will for my life. In Jesus Name I pray, Amen!

XIII

THANK GOD FOR THE BLOOD

"And they overcame him by the blood of the Lamb and by the word of their testimony and they loved not their lives unto death." (Rev. 12:11 –KJV)

According to the Scriptures, Jesus Christ, the Son of God, was betrayed by Judas Iscariot while in the Garden of Gethsemane. Matthew 26:48-49 declares:

"Now he that betrayed him gave them a sign, saying, whomsoever I shall kiss, that same is he: hold him fast. And forthwith he came to Jesus, and said, Hail, master; and kissed him." (KJV)

Pilate asked Jesus:

"Art thou the king of the Jews? And he answering said unto him, Thou sayest it." (Mark 15:2—KJV)" And he went again into the judgement hall, and saith unto Jesus, Whence art thou? But Jesus gave him no answer." (John 19:9—KJV) "Then Pilate said to him, speaketh thou not unto me, knowest thou not that I have power to crucify thee, and have power to release thee? Jesus answered, Thou couldest have no power at all against me, except it were given thee from above: therefore he that delivered me unto thee hath the greater sin." (John 19:10-11- KJV)

Pilate took Jesus and had him beaten. They whipped him, they blindfolded him and then they struck him on the face. They platted a crown of thorns and put it on his head. They also put a purple robe on him and mocked him saying "Hail king of the Jews".

Pilate then led Jesus out of the judgment hall. He said to the people *"I find in him no fault at all"* (John 18:38—KJV)

"Behold your king", Pilate said, but the people cried out, "take him away, we have no king but Caesar. Crucify him, crucify him" Then Pilate delivered Jesus to the people to be crucified.

When the soldiers had crucified Jesus, they took his garment and cast lots for it. They took a sponge filled with vinegar and they put it to his mouth. When Jesus had received the vinegar, he bowed his head and said *"it is finished" (John 19:30-KJV)*

The next day was the Sabbath. According to Jewish tradition, it was not lawful for the bodies to remain on the cross on the Sabbath day. So the soldiers came and broke the legs of the thieves who were hanging beside Jesus. But when they came to Jesus, they saw that he was dead already, and they did not break his legs. But one of the soldiers, took a spear and pierced his side and out came blood and water. (John 19:34)

Thank God for the blood!

Jesus left us a New Covenant. This Covenant replaced the Old Covenant. The Old Covenant stressed an eye for an eye, a tooth for a tooth and a life for a life. The New Covenant stressed love for thy neighbor, forgiveness and mercy.

In the Old Covenant, the priest went into the Holy of Holies once a year to make an atonement for the sins of the people. They offered the blood of goats, bulls, calves and turtledoves as a sacrifice for sin.

In the New Covenant, Jesus Christ entered one time into the Holy Place and offered His own blood to obtain eternal redemption for all of us. He offered Himself as a lamb without spot to God that He might purge us from all of those dead works. That He might cleanse us, make us holy, purify us and allow us to stand before His Father without shame. Jesus is the mediator of the New Covenant, which is His last will and Testament.

To become recipients of that last will and testament, there had to be a death involved. Blood had to be shed.

According to Hebrews 9:22:

"almost all things are by law purged with blood and without the shedding of blood, there is no remission for sin." (KJV)

In order for us to become heirs of the promise of eternal life, redemption and salvation, it was necessary that Christ enter into the Holy Place and die for us all. Our lives were stained with the filth of sin, guilt and shame.

There was no way that we could have saved ourselves. No avenue was open for us to escape the power and grip of sin. There was just no other route that could be taken other than through and by the shedding of blood.

Thank God for the blood!

Isaiah 53:5 declares:

"But he was wounded for our transgressions. He was bruised for our iniquities, the chastisement of our peace was upon him and with his stripes we are healed." (KJV)

Praise God, for we are healed by the wounds in his side. We are redeemed by the blood that he shed for us. Love came to the rescue and broke the chains of sin that had us shackled.

Romans 5:8,9 affirms:

"But God commendeth his love toward us, in that, while we were yet sinners, Christ died for us. Much more then, being justified by his blood, we shall be saved from wrath through Him." (KJV)

Because Christ died for us, we can stand before God justified (just as if we never sinned at all).

Thank God for the blood!

I Peter 1:18,19 states:

"For as much as ye know that ye were not redeemed with corruptible things such as silver and gold, from your vain conversations received by tradition form your fathers; but with the precious blood of Christ, as a lamb without blemish and without spot." (KJV)

The blood of goats and bulls could never take away sin. Idols of silver and gold could not redeem us. It took a lamb without spot and blemish to cleanse us from the awful stain of sin; Jesus is that lamb.

Revelation 12:7-11 proclaims:

"And there was war in heaven: Michael and his angels fought against the dragon; and the dragon fought and his angels, And prevailed not; neither was their place found any more in heaven.

And the great dragon was cast out, that old serpent, called the Devil, and Satan, which deceiveth the whole world: he was cast out into the earth, and his angels were cast out with him.

And I heard a loud voice saying in heaven, now is come salvation, and strength, and the kingdom of our God, and the power of his Christ: for the accuser of our brethren is cast down, which accused them before our God day and night,

And they overcame him by the blood of the Lamb, and by the word of their testimony; and they loved not their lives unto the death." (KJV)

My friends, there will come a day when Satan will be set free upon the earth to deceive the whole world, the only hope for the people on the earth will be to turn to Jesus and receive his blood of protection. Our scriptures tell us that the only way to overcome Satan is through and by the blood of Jesus Christ.

I Thessalonians 4:16-17 declares:

"For the Lord Himself shall descend from heaven with a shout, with the voice of the archangel and with the trump of God, and the dead in Christ shall rise first, then we which are alive and remain shall be caught up together with them in the clouds, to meet the Lord in the air and so shall we ever be with the Lord." (KJV)

Saints, we will be with the Lord, enjoying Him and His presence for all eternity. But millions of people will not have this privilege. Because they hardened their hearts to God and to His Word; they will remain on the earth to experience a time of great tribulation. Sin and sorrow, death and disease, pain and misery will run rampant. It will be a time such as the world has never known before.

Matthew 24:29-31 affirms:

"Immediately after the tribulation of those days shall the sun be darkened and the mon shall not give her light and the stars shall fall from heaven and the powers of the heavens shall be shaken.

And then shall appear the sign of the Son of man in heaven and they shall see the son of man coming in the clouds of heaven with power and great glory. And he shall send his angels with a great sound of a trumpet and they shall gather together his elect from the four winds from one end of the heaven to the other." (KJV)

Yes! Jesus will come again a second time as He came the first time and he will gather His people to Himself. The only seal of protection available will be the blood of Jesus. The only means of escape will be through and by the blood of Jesus. All of us, great and small, rich and poor, bond or free must stay under the blood of Jesus Christ our Savior and our Lord.

Hallelujah!

Amen!

Thank God for the blood!

Dear Heavenly Father,

Cleanse me and wash me with your blood that I may be able to stand before you free from sin. Forgive me for my sin. Place your seal of protection over my life that I may be counted worthy to escape the time of destruction and misery. Be with me though this life and forever. In Jesus' Name I pray. Amen!

XIV

LET GOD BE GOD FOR YOU

"No one is like you, Oh Lord, you are great and your name is mighty in power. But the Lord is the true God, he is the living God, the eternal King, when he is angry the earth trembles, the nations cannot endure His wrath." (Jeremiah 10:6,10—NIV)

In the Book of Jeremiah, we read about the people of God. They had turned their backs on the Lord and had begun to serve idols of wood, silver and gold. God spoke to his people. He called them back time and time again, but they would not listen. He reached out His hand to them. He appointed prophets over them to instruct them in His ways, but His people would not take heed to His commands.

God explicitly told His people:

"Thou shall have no other gods before me. Thou shalt not make unto thee any graven image...thou shalt not bow down thyself to them, nor serve them; for I the Lord thy God am a jealous God..." (Exo. 20:3-5-KJV)

The commandments were clear and understandable but Israel broke them over and over again. They served the gods of the other nations. They put up idols and bowed themselves down to them. They forgot about the one true God and they exchanged the glory of God for gods that were not gods at all.

Romans 1:21-25,28-32 tells the story of how Israel had abandoned the true God.

It declares:

"Because that when they knew God, they glorified Him not as God, neither were thankful, but became vain in their imaginations and their foolish heart was darkened.

Professing themselves to be wise, they became fools and changed the glory of the incorruptible God into an image made like unto corruptible man, and to birds, four-footed beast and creeping things.

Who changed the truth of God into a lie, and worshipped and served the creature more than the Creator, who is blessed forever Amen. And even as they did not like to retain God in their knowledge, God gave them over to a reprobate mind, to do those things which are not convenient;

Being filled with all unrighteousness, fornication, wickedness, covetousness, maliciousness; full of envy, murder, debate, deceit, malignity; whisperers, backbiters, haters of God, despiteful, proud, boasters, inventors of evil things, disobedient to parents, without understanding, covenant breakers, without natural affection, implacable, unmerciful:

Who knowing the judgement of God, that they which commit such things are worthy of death, not only do the same, but have pleasure in them that do them." (KJV)

When Aaron and the people worshipped the golden calf which they had made, God said to Moses:

"Go, get thee down; for thy people, which thou broughtest out of the land of Egypt, have corrupted themselves. They have turned aside quickly out of the way which I commanded them: they have made them a molten calf and have worshipped it, and have sacrificed thereunto,

and said, these be thy gods, O Israel, which have brought thee up out of the land of Egypt." (Exo. 32:7,8--KJV)

God's intent was to destroy all of them but Moses cried to the Lord and said:

"turn from thy fierce wrath and repent of this evil against thy people. Remember Abraham, Isaac and Israel thy servants." (Exo. 32:12,13—KJV)

Therefore, for the sake of a few righteous, holy and dedicated servants, God repented of *"the evil which he thought to do unto His people." (v.14)*

Nevertheless, those who committed this grave and despicable act had to be punished and their punishment was death. Exodus 32:28 affirms: that *"there fell of the people that day about three thousand men." (KJV)*

Three thousand people were slain that day, some by their brothers; some by their companions and others by their neighbors. After all that God had done for them, they took Him for granted and began to worship and serve other gods that could neither walk, talk nor deliver.

Time and time again they turned their backs on God. God again became angry with His people. He swore in His wrath to destroy them. He proclaimed that he would lay waste to the land, nothing would grow, no crops would flourish and His people would starve.

But in His great mercy, He relented and proclaimed that if they were to change their ways, repent and deal justly; if they were to put away the strange gods that stood before them, then and only then, would He come and stand before them and be their God.

You see, Israel thought that they could do without God. They failed over and over again because they did not take heed to his instructions. They rejected all of God's judgments and all of His commands. They refused to let God be their God.

Like Israel, the church too has failed God because we have not allowed God to God for us. We have not put God first in our lives. He is no longer a priority. We try and try to fix our lives, when we know that it is God whom we need to seek.

We struggle and struggle to manage our own affairs when we know that it is God who knows what is best for us. We cannot fix our problems and we cannot control our circumstances.

We must let God be God for us. He is the true God. He is the living God. He is the eternal King. There is no one like Him. He is great and His name is mighty in power. Let God Be God for you.

Dr. Sharon C. Cason

My Father, My King, My God,

I come to you with a humble heart and a bowed down head. I realize that there is no problem that is too difficult for you to solve. I take my heartaches, my disappointments and all of life's let downs and I place them in your hands. I am willing to trust you and I do believe that you will deliver me and give me total and complete victory. In Jesus' name, I pray Amen!

XV

I'M RUNNING FOR MY LIFE

"Know ye that they which run in a race run all, but one receiveth the prize? So run, that ye may obtain. And every man that striveth for the mastery is temperate in all things. Now they do it to obtain a corruptible crown, but we an incorruptible. I therefore so run, not as uncertainly, so fight I, not as one that beateth the air. But I keep under my body and bring it into subjection least that by any means, when I have preached to others, I myself should be a castaway." (I Cor. 9:24-27—KJV)

"Do you not know that in a race all runners run, but only one gets the prize? Run in such a way as to get the prize. Everyone who competes in the games goes into strict training. They do it to get a crown that will not last; but we do it to get a crown that will last forever. Therefore, I do not run like a man running aimlessly; I do not fight like a man beating the air. No, I beat my body and make it my slave so that after I have preached to others, I myself will not be disqualified for the prize." (NIV)

In the Scriptures, Apostle Paul declares to us that everyone who runs in a run, runs to receive a prize. In this Christian life, we too are running to receive a prize. Not a corruptible crown of silver or metal but a glorious incorruptible crown that will never decay or fade away.

Races were common in Corinth and the custom was to give a crown of leaves to the winner. This crown of leaves would eventually wither and decay.

But Apostle Paul pointed out the fact that we who are running in the Christian race, are not running to receive a crown of leaves. We are not running to get a reward that will decay, but all of us in this spiritual journey, are running for our lives. We are running to get a crown of eternal life. We are not in competition with our sisters and brothers. It's not about me getting to the finish line before you nor you getting there before me. It is all about whether we are running the race in such a way that we will receive a crown of victory.

The rules of running a race are quite simple and very clear:

- **First:**
  The runners line up at the starting point and when the gun is fired, they take off immediately. There is no time to stand around wondering what just happened. When we give our hearts to Christ, we must be ready to start the race immediately. We must be like Apostle Paul when he was on the road to Damascus.
  He said *"Lord what will thou have me to do."* (Acts 9:5— KJV) When Paul received his sight, he was with the disciples at Damascus for many days. After that, Acts 9:20 declares: *"and straightway he preached Christ in the synagogues, that he is the Son of God." (KJV)*

- **Second:**
  The runners must stay on the track and stay in his or her own lane until the race is completed. It's very important to stay on the track and it is equally important to stay in your lane. You can't stop running to see what others are doing and you cannot interfere with anyone else's race. You must stay on the track, take care of your business and stay in your own lane until the race is over. The problem comes in when we interfere with our sisters and

brothers. We are admonished to exalt each other every day and not to hinder, come against or cause division in anyone's life.

In I Corinthians 15:58 Apostle Paul affirmed:
Therefore, my beloved brethren, be ye steadfast, unmovable, always abounding in the work of the Lord for as much as ye know that your labor is not in vain in the Lord.* *"(KJV)

- **Third:**
  In running a race, the runner cannot be distracted by the crowd. He cannot look back to see where the other runners are. He must not stop to pick daisies along the way. He must persevere until he reaches the finish line.
  Isaiah 40:31 declares:
  "But they that wait upon the Lord shall renew their strength, they shall mount up with wings as eagles, they shall run and not be weary and they shall walk and not faint." (KJV)
  When you finish running a race, they tell you to walk it off. Don't faint! Don't sit down! Don't fall out! God is telling us that same thing. When we run this race of life, we must wait on direction, wait on guidance and wait on the power of the Holy Spirit and God will give us more strength and more endurance. We shall mount up with wings. We shall run and not fall out and when we are done, then we can just walk it off. Hallelujah!

- **Fourth:**
  The runner must lay aside everything that will hinder him from winning the race. His main focus must be on victory. His mind and body must be physically disciplined in order to accomplish the task and reach his goal. When a runner runs, he wears light clothing. He takes off everything that could slow him down. He disciplines his body. He disciplines his mind. His mind is on the race. He says to himself, I can do this, I am a winner, I am strong and I am a survivor. Likewise, the Christian must constantly remind himself—I can do all things through Christ who gives me strength. I can be who God wants me to be. I can do what God

wants me to do. I am more than a conqueror through Christ Jesus my Lord. The runner must be willing to set aside all his worldly goals and ambitions for the cause of Christ.

In verse 26, of I Corinthians the 9th chapter, Paul says *"I therefore so run, not as uncertainly."*
In other words, he is saying, I know why I'm running. I'm not uncertain. I am not indecisive. I'm not double minded. I'm not as one who is beating the air. I'm not one who is running just for the sake of running. But my aim is higher ground, my eyes are on the prize of eternal life. Then Paul says, I keep my body under subjection.
Paul was saying that he was completely committed, dedicated, consecrated and separated. I am running for my life.

I Peter 4:4 says: *"Wherein they think it strange that ye run not with them to the same excess of riot, speaking evil of you." (KJV)*

There will be those who wonder why you are running for God as you are. They may ask you such questions as:

- Why are you always praying?
- Why are you always in church?
- What's wrong with that church over there?

But you must stay consistent. You must say to them that you are doing what you need to do to run this Christian race and to finish your course. Paul says in Galatians 2:2: *"lest by any means I should run or had run in vain." (KJV)*
We don't want to run this race in vain.
We don't want to get to the end of the race and fall out. We must walk it off.
We must walk off all the lies that have been told about us. We must walk off all the rumors that have been spread.
Yes, walk off all the sickness and pain that we had to endure.

Walk off all the gossip and hurtful things that have been said and walk off all the tests and trials that we had to go through.
Hallelujah!
Praise God!
We must tell the enemy to leave us alone because we are running for our lives.

Heavenly Father, in the name of Jesus,

We ask for strength to continue running this race of life. We thank you because you have allowed us to run this race in spite of the obstacles and barriers that have been placed in our way. Forgive us for slacking up or slowing down and help us to persevere regardless to the circumstances. We thank you for the victory. Amen!

•

XVI

YES, GOD REALLY DOES LOVE US

"Behold, what manner of live the Father hath bestowed upon us that we should be called the sons of God..." (I John 3:1—KJV)

"God loves you". These are three simple words, so simple and yet so true. People say it all the time. It's written on bill boards, it's painted on signs and even written on t-shirts. But I wonder if anyone really knows how much God loves them?

- First, let's explain what God's love entails. God's love is directed to us, unworthy objects, purely because He desires it to be. Our scripture verse in I John 3:1 declares that God has bestowed His love upon us so that we can be called His children. The word bestowed *"suggests the enduring effect of the love God has given" (The King James Study Bible* notes) This simply means that God's love keeps on giving and giving and giving. There is no end to the love of God.

- Second—Let us consider the phrase "God is love".
  I John 4:8 affirms: **"He that loveth not knoweth not God; for God is love." (KJV)**
  God's love for mankind can only be manifested through His grace, mercy, kindness and favor.
  I John 4:16 states:

> *"And we have known and believed the love that God hath to us. God is love; and he that dwelleth in love dwelleth in God and God in him." (KJV)*

- Thirdly—Let us look at the phrase—"Love in action"
Love can only be known from the action it prompts. God's love for mankind is seen in the gift of His Son.
I John 3:16 sates:

> *"This is how we know what love is: Jesus Christ laid down his life for us..." (NIV)* I John 4:9-10 further declare: *"This is how God showed his love among us: He sent his one and only Son into the world that we might live through him. This is love: not that we love God, but that he loved us and sent his son as an atoning sacrifice for our sins (NIV)*

Again I say, yes, God really does love us!

All of us are in need of God's help, God's mercy and His grace. The Bible explains in Romans 3:23:

"For all have sinned and come short of the glory of God." (KJV) Even King David exclaimed in Psalm 51:5:

"Behold, I was shapen in iniquity and in sin did my mother conceive me. "(KJV)

So, if we were conceived in sin, shaped in our mother's womb to be born in sin, then why does God love us so?

We all were sinking in sin. All of us were unclean, defiled and unholy human beings; who could never deserve God's love or His kindness, but He loves us anyway.

According to Isaiah 64:4, even the little good that we try to do, the little righteous thing which we press toward, are counted as filthy dirty rags that you take and throw in the garbage. But God loves us anyway.

In the 14th chapter of Job and the 6th verse, Job asks a question.

He says:

"Who can bring a clean thing out of an unclean? (KJV)

And to that question, I answer no one, no one except God. We were all unclean, unrighteous and unholy. Jesus Christ wiped our slate clean.

Isaiah 1:18 exhorts*:*

"Come now and let us reason together, saith the Lord: though your sins be as scarlet they shall be white as snow; though they be red like crimson, they shall be as wool." (KJV)

We cannot cleanse ourselves. We must accept the cleansing offered to us by the Lord Jesus. We must come together in agreement with the Father and allow His cleansing agent to wash us white as snow. Here the Father is extending to all men a sacred invitation.

He says "come" and "come now". Your sins which are presently "red like crimson" (meaning stained from the guilt and condemnation of sin) can now become snowy white (meaning clean, pure and holy). Have you ever looked out of your window after a snow fall? If you have you would have seen the brightness and pureness of new fallen snow.

Everything feels fresh and new. All around you there is a pleasant smell in the air. Taking a breath in this type of snow is like breathing the very air of heaven. God loves us so much that he wants to take the filthiness of sin and turn it into the pureness of new fallen snow.

Hallelujah!

That's a lot to be thankful for.

God the Father, sent his son to redeem us, justify us and make us whole. In chapter 13 and verse 23 of the book bearing his name, Jeremiah asks three questions:

1. Can the Ethiopian change his skin?
2. Can the leopard change his spots?
3. Can you do good when you are accustomed to doing evil?

The *answers* are no, no and no. Only God our father can bring about a change in us and He does it so that we will know just how much He really loves us.

The people of God have fallen short of His glory. They missed the mark. The things that should have done, they did not do. The people of God grieved God to his heart. They made him angry and even made him repent that he had ever made man and yet God continued to love them. In desiring to annihilate all human beings, the love of God instead prompted Noah to build an ark in yet another desperate attempt to save man.

The words of this song entitled "How He loves Me", written by John Mark MacMillan, explains just how rich God's love is for us. The first stanza says: *"He is jealous for me. His love is like a hurricane and I am a tree, bending beneath the weight of his wind and mercy."* You see, God's love completely engulfs us and there is no way we can get away from it. It does not matter who we are of what we done in life, His love has touched all of us in some form. Being jealous over us is God's way of saying that He loves us so much that he does not want us to put anything nor anyone before Him.

The next stanza says: *"when all of a sudden, I am unaware of these afflictions eclipsed by His glory, I realize just how beautiful you are and how great your affections are for me."* I know that I have done wrong. I know that I have gone the wrong way but His glory is all over me and one day a light comes on in my head and I come to the realization of just how great His affections are for me. I see that He truly, truly loves me and I do not remember the sin anymore because I am eclipsed by His glory. I am shielded from the misery of sin by the glory of God.

Another stanza reads: *"We are His portion, He is our prize, we are drawn to redemption by the grace in his eyes, if grace is an ocean then we are all sinking."* Praise God! We are all sinking in His grace. He drew us to Himself with cords of love. He redeemed us. He set us free and we are all sinking in His grace. We are all surrounded by His grace.

Think about your life. Think about how you deserved death for the sins that you committed. We all deserved the death penalty. We did not deserve God's grace. We could never be good enough and we can never do enough good; but God looked on us with grace in his eyes and He declared through His Word:

"Father forgive them"

"Father save them"

"I will purchase their salvation"

"I will shed my blood for them"

"I will die for mankind"

The last stanza of the song says: *"Oh how he loves us, yes, he loves us"*

"Because of the Lord's great love we are not consumed, for his compassions fail not." (Lamentations 3:22--NIV)

"Greater love has no one than this, that he lay down his life for His friends. (John 15:13—NIV)

Some of us have done a lot of things we should not have. Many of us have brought God to an open shame and the majority of us have used the name of God in an unholy manner. But we don't have time to go back down memory lane. We don't have time to maintain regrets. We must think about how much God loves us here and now.

Dear Heavenly Father,

Please open my eyes that I may see just how much you love me. Help me to draw nearer to you every single day realizing that I could never repay you for what you have done for me. I thank You for your mercy, for your grace and most of all for your love. I love you Lord! Amen!

XVII

STAND BY ME LORD

"For there stood by me this night the angel of God, whose I am, and whom I serve, saying, fear not, Paul; thou must be brought before Caesar: and, lo, God hath given thee all them that sail with thee." (Acts 27:23-24—KJV)

The Apostle Paul is one of the greatest apostles in the New Testament. By his own testimony, he said that he was a persecutor of the Christians.

He went from place to place and from house to house pulling men and women out of their homes to be imprisoned, whipped, chained and even beheaded.

But Paul said, that one day while he was on the Damascus road, on his way to persecute the Christians, that a bright light flashed from heaven and he heard a voice from heaven saying:

"Saul, Saul, why persecuteth thou me?"

Paul said that he fell to the ground and asked, who are you Lord? The voice answered

"I am Jesus whom thou persecuteth. It is hard for thee to kick against the pricks." (Acts 9:4,5—KJV)

Trembling with fear, Paul immediately said to Jesus:

"Lord what will thou have me to do?" Jesus said to Paul— *"Arise and go into the city and it will be told to thee what thou must do." (Acts 9:6—KJV)*

Paul said that he arose from the earth and when he opened his eyes he could not see. The men that were with him, took him by the hand and led him into the city. He was 3 days and 3 nights without food and without sight.

In the city, there was a certain disciple dwelling there by the name of Ananias.

The Lord said to Ananias:

"Arise, go into the street which is called Straight and enquire in the house of Judas for a man called Saul of Tarsus, for, behold he prayeth and hath seen in a vision a man named Ananias coming in and putting his hand on him that he might receive his sight." (Acts 9:11,12---KJV)

Ananias said to Jesus:

"Lord, I have heard by many of this man, how much evil he hath done to the saints at Jerusalem. And here he hath authority from the chief priests to bind all that call on thy name" (Acts 9:13,14)

But Jesus said to Ananias:

"Go your way, for he is a chosen vessel to me, to bear my name before the Gentiles, and before kings and the children of Israel. For I will show him how great things he must suffer for my name's sake." (Acts. (:15,16—KJV)

Ananias went to Paul and when he entered the house, he laid his hands on Paul saying:

"Brother Saul, the Lord, even Jesus, that appeared unto thee in the way as thou camest, hath sent me that thou mightiest receive thy sight, and be filled with the Holy Ghost." (Acts 9:17—KJV)

The Bible says in verse 18:

"immediately, there fell from his eyes as if it had been scales and he received his sight, forthwith, and arose and was baptized" (KJV)

Paul then began to preach in the synagogues that Jesus is the Son of God.

Paul increased more and more in the power of the Lord, so much so that the Jews tried to kill him. They watched the city gates day and night trying to trap him and kill him.

When he came to Jerusalem, the disciples were afraid of him and did not believe that he was now one of them. That did not stop Paul however, he spoke boldly in the name of Jesus but many still sought to kill him.

Later, Paul wrote in the Book of Corinthians 11:23-27 that he had been beaten above measure. He was in prison frequently and in death often.

He said:

"of the Jews five times received I forty stripes save one. Thrice was I beaten with rods, once was I stoned, thrice I suffered shipwreck, a night and a day I have been in the deep; in journeyings often, in perils of water, in perils of robbers, in perils by mine own countrymen, in perils by the heathen, in perils in the city, in perils in the wilderness, in perils in the sea, in perils among false brethren; in weariness and painfulness, in watchings often, in hunger and thirst, in fastings often, in cold and nakedness." (KJV)

Yes, Paul did suffer many hardships and now we see Apostle Paul in the 26th chapter of Acts, standing before King Agrippa, testifying to how Jesus of Nazareth appointed him to be a servant and a minister to the Gentiles.

"To open their eyes, to turn them from darkness to light, and from the power of Satan to the power of God, that they may receive forgiveness of sins, an inheritance among them which are sanctified by faith that is in me." (Acts 26:18—KJV)

Festus the governor shouted at Paul saying:

"Paul thou art beside thyself, much learning doth make thee mad, (Acts 26:24—KJV)

But King Agrippa said to Paul ---*"Almost thou persuadeth me to be a Christian" (Acts 26:28—KJV)*

When they could do nothing against Paul, they sent him to Caesar.

When the men set sail to Rome, Paul declared to them that there would be a lot of damage and loss to the ship, but no one took heed to Paul's words.

While on the way to Rome, a storm came on the sea with hurricane winds and Paul and the men on the ship were caught in the storm. Being caught in the storm, the men on board began to panic because the ship was being tossed to and from by the winds and waves.

The storm was so violent that the next day, the men began to lighten the ship and they threw out the cargo. They threw out the food.

They threw out anything that was weighting the ship down. On the third day, they threw out the tackle.

When neither sun nor stars appeared for many days and the storm raged on, they gave up all hope of ever being saved. The wind blew on, the storm raged on, the rain poured down. There was no help in sight.

Paul said:

"sirs ye should have hearkened unto me and not have loosed from Crete (Acts 27:21—KJV).

Then Paul stood in the midst of the ship and said:

"I exhort you to be of good cheer, there shall be no loss of any man's life among any of you, but of the ship, for there stood by me this night an angel of God, whom I am and whom I serve, saying, fear not, Paul, thou must be brought to Caesar and lo, God hath given thee all them that sail with thee" (Acts 27:23,24—KJV)

Despite Paul's encouraging words, the men on board the ship could not see any hope in sight. Day after day, the storm raged on. Night after night, the winds continued to blow.

The ship was driven and tossed by the waves. As the ship was being pushed into the rocks, water was filling the ship. The shipmen panicked again, they let down the anchors and cut off the ropes. Some of them had purposed to jump overboard but Paul said to them:

"except these abide in the ship, ye cannot be saved (Acts 27:31—KJV)

The storm continued for many days and nights until the ship ran aground and was broken by the violent waves.

The soldiers decided to kill the prisoners before they escaped, but the centurion commanded them not to do it because he knew that Paul was a man of God. Everyone began to jump into the sea.

Those who could swim, cast themselves into the sea. The rest were on boards. Some were on broken pieces of the ship but all of them came safely to land just as the angel of God had said.

If you are in a spiritual storm today, if that storm is tossing you like a ship on the sea. Know that your Heavenly Father **WILL** stand by you.

Dear Heavenly Father,

Please be our guide in times of distress and hopelessness. Let us know that you alone will be our help in times of trouble. Help us to see your glory in everything that we do or say. Thank you for standing by us in the past and thank you for continuing to stand by us now. We praise you to the highest. Hallelujah! Amen!

XVIII

LET THE BLESSINGS BREAK FORTH

"Sing, O barren, thou that didst not bear, break forth into singing, and cry aloud, thou that didst not travail with child: for more are the children of the desolate than the children of the married wife, saith the Lord. Enlarge the place of thy tent and let them stretch forth the curtains of thine habitation; spare not, lengthen thy stakes...for thou shalt break forth on the right hand and on the left." (Isaiah 54:1-3—KJV)

In this text, we read about the people of God and the city of God (Jerusalem). At this point, Jerusalem had been barren and fruitless. The walls had been torn down, the city had been burnt and God's people had been exiled because of their disobedience. The people of God were ashamed of their situation. They were in fear and disgrace. They felt as if their captivity would continue forever.

But here we read how God is encouraging the exiles through the prophet Isaiah, by promising new conditions that would bring blessings and joy. Though they were afflicted and distressed now, God promised a time of peace, righteousness and glory. In knowing that this time was at hand, they were admonished to break forth with singing and to cry aloud with shouts of joy.

The people of God did cry but their cries were not joyful cries. They were in bondage. They were in pain and they cried like a woman in labor. A mother in labor may cry out, scream or even yell at the hospital staff assisting her and maybe even at her husband.

Consider a husband in the labor room with his wife. Imagine him holding her hand during the birth of their child. Maybe both of them are crying. The mother is crying because of the trauma and birth pains she is experiencing. The husband is crying because he empathizes with his wife. But after the child is born, there is another type of crying and it is a cry of joy. This is the type of crying that God gave to Israel and this is what God is giving to His people today.

In order to receive this type of joy, we must prepare ourselves for these blessings. In verse 2, God tells us 5 things that we must do:

First God said: **Enlarge the place of thy tent** ----God was telling Israel to enlarge the place of their tents because they were about to bring forth a multitude of children which they did not have to labor for. They needed to be able to hold this great multitude that would soon flock to them.

We, as the people of God, must come out of our comfort zones to reach those who need us. If we are looking for a great blessing from God, we need to be diligent and serve God with all of our heart.

Jesus commanded the disciples in Matthew 10:5,6:

"do not go into the way of the Gentiles and do not go into the city of the Samaritans, but go rather to the lost sheep of the house of Israel" (KJV)

They were to go to their own people first. We too, must fulfill the command of God and go to our own family first with the Word of God. We must tell them about the love of God.

John 1:40-42 declares:

"One of the two which heard John speak, and followed him, was Andrew, Simon Peter's brother. He first findeth his own brother Simon

and saith unto him, we have found the Messiah…and he brought him to Jesus…" (KJV)

After the death and resurrection of Jesus, the work of redemption was complete, and He exalted His disciples to:

"Go ye therefore and teach all nations" (Matthew 28:19, KJV)

NOW, their goal was to go into all the world and preach the Gospel to all people.

That is the responsibility of the church. Jesus commissioned the disciples in Acts 1:8 to be witnesses in Jerusalem, in Judea, in Samaria and unto the uttermost parts of the earth.

No longer were they confined to a certain group of people, to a certain nationality or class of people, their tents were enlarged to include all people.

It is therefore, up to us to do the same. We must enlarge the place of our tents so that we can reach as many people as we can with the Word of God.

Second, God said—**Stretch forth the curtains of thine habitations.**

Sometimes, we can't see what we are to be or do because our spiritual curtains are closed. We can't see on the outside. We can only see on the inside. We see our own problems. We see our own situation. We see what we need and what we want, but we cannot see the needs of others because our curtains are closed.

You may be able to hear the rain but when your curtains are closed, you can't see the sunshine. You can't see that it's getting better all the time.

With your curtains closed, you hear the thunder and lightning but you can't see the rainbow after the storm. You can't see that a brighter day has already come.

The curtains could also represent the eyes of the soul. A lot of times we close our eyes to other people because we are so absorbed in our own world and our own problems.

Romans 11:8-10 affirms that God gave Israel the spirit of slumber. Their eyes were darkened so that they could not see and their ears were dull and they could not hear.

They were a snare and a stumbling block to themselves. They were their own worst enemy. Israel was given for our example that we will not follow after their pattern of living.

Psalm 19:1 states:

"The heavens declare the glory of God, and the firmament showest his handiwork." (KJV)

We need to open our eyes so that we may see the wonders that God have created. We need to stretch forth the curtains of our habitation and behold the mighty works of God.

Have you ever gone to the window and just peeped out? That is what a lot of people are doing. They are going to church faithfully but they are only peeping out to the world. They are singing in the choir faithfully but they are only peeping out to those who really need the Word. You cannot enjoy a rainbow until you go outside.

A lot of us stay inside and only peep out when it snows. But to fully enjoy the beauty of the snow, we have to go outside and walk in it or play in it or just breathe in the fresh new scent that a snow fall brings with it. That is what God is saying to all of us today, stretch forth the curtains of your habitation and then you will be able to see the great things that God has waiting for you.

Third God says—**<u>Spare Not</u>**

When Israel went into the land of promise, they were instructed by God to utterly destroy the enemy. Wipe them out and spare no one. They were not to make a league with the enemy. Because if they did, their enemy would surely be a snare to them. Yet they failed to pray and seek God. They entered into a covenant with the enemy that they could not break. (Joshua 9:1-6)

Now, they had people who served idol gods were right in the midst of them and Israel soon took on the ways of the enemy and forgot about God.

In I Samuel the 15th chapter, we read that God told King Saul:

"go and smite Amalek and utterly destroy all that they have, slay both man and woman, infant and child, sheep and oxen, camel and donkey, and spare them not." (KJV)

But Saul spared the best of the sheep and he also spared the King of Amalek. It was Saul's responsibility to destroy the Amalekites and to completely wipe out their evil ways.

The Amalekites had been a snare to God's people in the past and if they were not destroyed they would continue to be so in the future. When Israel was coming out of Egypt, the Amalekites came behind them and killed the weak and the feeble, the old men and the sick ones.

The Amalekites were descendants of Esau and even though Jacob and Esau reconciled as brothers, their descendants did not. God blessed Joshua and the Israelites to defeat the Amalekites at that time. As long as Moses' hands were held up, the Israelites were victorious against the Amalekites. Now, here they are again and King Saul must destroy them but he does not obey God.

We all know that there are things that we need to get rid of. We need to let those thing go before they destroy us. We must be obedient to God because He knows what is best for us. Sometimes, there are people we need to separate ourselves from.

Our right hand is offending us but we won't let it go. There are some things that we need to rid ourselves of if we want to break forth into our blessings.

Don't spare the enemy. We must rebuke him at all costs. We should not make an agreement with the devil but cast him out instead.

Isaiah 58:1 declares:

"cry aloud, spare not, lift up thy voice like a trumpet and show my people their transgressions and the house of Israel their sins." (KJV)

Be a bold soldier for God. Cry out for God. Lift up your voice like a trumpet blast. We must cry out against sin and not allow the devil to win.

Fourth God says---**Lengthen thy cords**

Cords were used in the Old Testament, to tie the tents down. Without the cords, the tents were unstable. In order to get the tent secured and stable, sometimes the cords had to be lengthened. This was done to offer a greater surface to the storms, to spread out more canvas and to cover more ground. How do you lengthen a cord that's too short for the job that you need to do? You add more to it by tying and binding it together.

In binding the cords together to erect the tent, sometimes the cords would break and the job had to be started all over again. To avoid that problem, they had to tie the cord in twos and threes.

According to Ecclesiastes 4:12:

"a three-fold cord is not easily broken." (KJV)

What is God saying to us today? He is saying that we need each other. We have to lengthen our cords and the only way we can do that is to get with some strong saints who are able to lift us up and help us get to where God desires us to be.

It does not matter who we are in the Lord or who we think we are. We will always need a stronger, wiser and more experience child of God to help us. A three-fold cord is not easily broken. One alone can be broken. Two might be stronger but also can be broken. But 3 together cannot be easily broken.

You cannot stand by yourself. You are going to need someone to pray for you, to encourage you and to hold you up in times of crisis. When the wind is blowing and the storms are raging, just lengthen your cords.

Ecclesiastes 4:9-12 states:

"Two are better than one, because they have a good reward for their labor. For if they fall, the one will lift up his fellow: but woe to him that is alone when he falleth; for he hath not another to help him up. Again, if two lie together, then they have heat, but how can one be warm alone? And if one prevail against him, two shall withstand him, and a three-fold cord is not easily broken." (KJV)

Fifth, God says---**Strengthen thy stakes**

When a tent is erected, the stakes have to be placed securely in the ground so that the tent does not collapse. If the stakes are too weak, you must get bigger, better and stronger ones. If the stakes are too weak, your shelter will be swept away by the storms. It is sad to say that some of our spiritual tents have toppled over because of increased winds and rain storms.

It is a terrible thing to have your tent fall down during a storm. The foundation was weak and your stakes were not deeply rooted and grounded into the Word of God.

So here God tells us to strengthen our stakes. We cannot fall apart over every small problem. We must be strong in the Lord and the power of his might. We must stand firm, my friends. We cannot allow trouble and heartaches to move us so easily. We have to get a sure grip on God and strengthen our stakes.

There is an old hymn that says--:" *on Christ the solid rock I stand; all other ground is sinking sand"*

We have to get a sure grip on Jesus Christ or our spiritual tents will fall. We must put more prayer in our day and put more of God's word in our heart. It is so shocking to see how people take prayer and Bible Study so lightly. When the storms of life come along they quickly fall by the wayside because Bible Study and Prayer service was not important to them.

Isaiah 55:10-12 states:

"For as the rain cometh down, and the snow from heaven, and returneth not thither, but watereth the earth and maketh it bring forth and bud, that it may give seed to the sower, and bread to the eater, so shall my word be that goeth forth out of my mouth, it shall not return unto me void, but it shall accomplish that which I please and it shall prosper in the thing whereto I sent it.

For ye shall go out with joy and be led forth with peace: the mountains and the hills shall break forth before you into singing and all the trees of the field shall clap their hands." (KJV)

What is God saying to us?

God is telling us that soon we will break forth on every side.

He wants us to prepare ourselves for the fierce winds and angry tempest that are going to come our way. God is admonishing us through the Prophet Isaiah to get ready because greater, stronger and mightier, miraculous blessings are on the way.

Hallelujah!

Dr. Sharon C. Cason

Dear God,

Please give me peace through all of my trials and tests, that I may be a stronger and mightier child for you. Help me to tie all my cords together and make all my stakes stronger that I may hold out until you return for me. Amen!

XIX

DON'T LOSE YOUR DREAM

"When the Lord turned again the captivity of Zion, we were like them that dream. Then was our mouth filled with laughter, and our tongue with singing: then, said they among the heathen, The Lord hath done great things for them. The Lord hath done great things for us; whereof we are glad. Turn again our captivity, O Lord, as the streams in the south. They that sow in tears shall reap in joy. He that goeth forth and weepeth, bearing precious seed, shall doubtless come again with rejoicing, bringing his sheaves with him." (Psalm 126)

Do you have a dream? A deep, deep desire imbedded inside of you? Are you longing to do more or to be more for God?

Dreams causes you to create what you believe or what you imagine. Your dreams represent your inner desires. When you dream and dream big, you are fulfilled right to the soul because you are seeking out your true purpose in life.

Israel had a dream.

They had been taken into captivity because of their rebellion against God. The people of Jerusalem had sinned grievously, therefore, they were removed from the place of honor and from the position of glory. All the people cried.

Their pleasant things were gone. Their sanctuary had been desecrated, burned and torn down. The enemy had taken full control of everything. Even their kings, in which they trusted, were taken captive to Babylon.

Their prophets were chained, bound and put in prison. All of their gold, silver and precious things were gone.

The Lord was angry with Israel and He, Himself, became their enemy.

Instead of fighting for them, He fought against them. He destroyed all their strongholds and took away their tabernacles. He allowed their captives to destroy their places of assembly and God, Himself, despised their solemn feasts and Sabbaths.

God purposely stretched out his hand against them and their false gods. Their hearts cried out unto the Lord. Their tears ran down like a river, day and night. They cried morning, noon and night.

They poured out their hearts to the Lord. Their women prayed. The priests and the prophets cried out to the Lord. The young and the old laid on the ground in the streets. They called out to God saying—remember us, save us, help us; but God would not hear their prayer.

Lamentations 3: states:

"He hath hedged me about that I cannot get out: he hath made my chain heavy."(KJV) He filled them with bitterness, misery and pain.

But they had a dream.

They knew that they had done wrong.

But they had a dream.

They knew that they had forsaken the true God and provoked him to anger by serving other gods.

But in spite of their circumstances, they had a dream.

They dreamed that God would restore them and turn their captivity around. They had hope that even though God was angry with them, that his anger would only endure for a moment. The tears that they shed were multiplied greatly but they knew that their weeping would endure for only and night and that joy surely would come in the morning.

Jeremiah was one of the prophets who were taken into captivity with Israel. He saw their misery firsthand. He saw their pain and he suffered with them. Whatever they experienced, he experienced. When they cried, he cried. Because Israel's heart was broken, Jeremiah's heart was broken as well.

Jeremiah described their plight in the Book of Lamentations, chapter 3:

> ➢ I am the man that hath seen affliction by the rod of his wrath—v. 1
> ➢ He hath led me and brought me into darkness—v. 3
> ➢ My flesh and my skin hath he broken—v. 4
> ➢ He hath set me in dark places—v. 6
> ➢ I cry and shout, he shuts out my prayer—v. 8
> ➢ He hath turned aside my ways and pulled me in pieces—v. 11
> ➢ He hath bent his bow and set me as a mark for the arrow—v. 12
> ➢ He hath filled me with bitterness-v. 15

Jeremiah' hope was gone and his soul was in affliction.

But Jeremiah had a dream.

He remembered how good and merciful God had been to Israel and he encouraged the people by declaring:

"Because of the Lord's great love we are not consumed, for his compassions never fail. They are new every morning: great is your faithfulness. I say to myself, the Lord is my portion; therefore, I will wait for him. The Lord is good to those whose hope is in him, to the one who seeks him; it is good to wait quietly for the salvation of the Lord.

It is good for a man to bear the yoke while he is young." (Lamentations 3:22-27-NIV)

Jeremiah told the people that they should have been destroyed by the enemy and they did not have to let them live but because God was still merciful, loving and compassionate, they are still alive. He has not wiped them out completely.

Then Jeremiah exclaims:

" for men are not cast off by the Lord forever. Though he brings grief, he will show compassion, so great is his unfailing love. For he does not willingly bring affliction or grief to the children of men. (Lamentations 3:31-33-NIV)

Jeremiah exalted the people by saying:

"let us examine our ways and test them and let us return to the Lord. Let us lift up our hearts and our hands to God in heaven and say: We have sinned and rebelled and you have not forgiven." (Lamentations 3:40-42-NIV)

What Jeremiah was saying in essence was; Let us dream again. We have transgressed and rebelled against the Lord, but let's go back and ask God for mercy. Let's confess our sins so he will forgive us. Let us dream.

That is the point that I am attempting to convey to you today; let us dream again.

If you have a dream, pursue it.

Don't lose your dream, follow it.

Don't let problems and adversity keep you from realizing your dream.

All of my life, I have had a desire to write a book. Many things prevented the completion and even the process of getting started. I took many wrong paths and came face to face with difficulties and pain. I was ready to give up on my dream.

I also wanted to have a Bible College and God blessed that dream to come to fruition, but the book was still unfinished and unpublished.

I started the process over and over again, struggling to find the right words to write down. It looked as if my dream would soon die, but one day, the Holy Spirit spoke to my heart and encouraged me to finish the book.

The book that you now hold is my dream being made alive and full.

When you dream, doors will be opened for you.

When you dream, you will achieve greatness.

When you dream, you can accomplish things that you never thought you would.

We cannot focus on life's problems.

We cannot let the lack of money deter us.

We must not let the enemy keep us from dreaming.

There are many people who will not see your dream. They may hinder your progress by speaking negative words on your life but do not let that worry you. If the dream is in you, then it is real and one day the world will see the dream that God placed within you being realized.

Joseph had a dream. It was a seemingly impossible dream. He dreamed that one day, the sun, the moon and the 11 stars would bow down to him.

Genesis 37:10 declares:

"When he told his father as well as his brothers, his father rebuked him and said, what is this dream you had? Will your mother and I

and your brothers actually come and bow down to the ground before you? His brothers were jealous of him, but his father kept the matter in mind." (NIV)

Joseph's brothers hated him and envied him but his father observed him, knowing that there was a deeper meaning to the dream. Joseph's father realized that the hand of God was upon his son.

Before Joseph's dream was manifested, however, he had to face great adversity, great sorrow and disappointment. He was put into a pit and sold into slavery, all by the hands of his brothers.

While in Egypt, he was falsely accused and put into prison for 2 years. But Joseph never lost sight of his dream and neither should you.

Martin Luther King, Jr, had a dream. On August 23, 1963 he verbalized his dream, on the steps of the Lincoln Memorial in Washington DC., to thousands of people waiting and fighting for freedom, justice and equality.

He declared:

"Even though we face the difficulties of today and tomorrow I still have a dream.

It is a dream deeply rooted in the American dream. I have a dream that one day this nation will rise up and live out the true meaning of its creed: "we hold these truths to be self-evident; that all men are created equal.

I have a dream that one day on the red hills of Georgia the sons of former slaves and the sons of former slave owners will be able to sit together at the table of brotherhood.... I have a dream that little children will one day live in a nation where they will not be judged by the color of their skin but by the content of their character, I have a dream today." (www.analytictech.com)

Yes, Martin Luther King Jr had a dream.

It was a seemingly insurmountable dream. But it has been realized in you and I today. He was jailed, beaten, attacked and finally shot down by one who never wanted the dream to come to fruition.

Despite of the obstacles he faced, he was not afraid to dream big and his dream lives on in us.

Langston Hughes, the great Harlem renaissance poet, was a dreamer too. He wrote a poem entitled: **I Dream a World**

He wrote:

I dream a world where man
No other man will scorn,
Where love will bless the earth
And peace its path adorn
I dream a world where all
Will know sweet freedom's way
Where greed no longer saps the soul
Nor avarice blights our day

When we dream, we open our hearts up to so many possibilities. We can dream of goodness. We can dream of spiritual freedom, physical freedom of just of the freedom that holds our minds captive.

A world I dream where black and white,
Whatever race may be,
Will share the bounties of the earth
And every man is free,
Where wretchedness will hang its head
And joy, like a pearl
Attends the needs of all mankind-
Of such I dream, my world.

(https://allpoetry.com)

We can also dream of problems that face humanity and wonder who will be the one to correct the errors of mistakes made centuries ago. What can be done so that all of us, feel the life sustaining breath that God intended for all of us, not some of us. A dream takes you far beyond reality into a world yet to be but not impossible to be.

My friends, what is going to happen to your dream? Langston Hughes again wrote so eloquently by stating:

What happens to a dream deferred?
Does it dry up like a raisin in the sun?
Or fester like a sore and then run?
Does it stink like rotten meat?
Or crust and sugar over like syrupy sweet?
Maybe it just sags like a heavy load.
Or does it explode?

(Deferred Dream Selected poems of Langton Hughes, Random House Inc. 1990)

Don't let your dream explode.

Don't let it weigh on you like a heavy load.

No, reach toward your dream and if it has died, resurrect it in Jesus name. Amen!

Dear Lord,

Thank you for all the dreams that you have placed within me. My desire is to realize how blessed I truly am to have a mind and a heart to dream. Give me the patience to wait upon my dream and to see it come to fruition. I pray in Jesus name. Amen!

Are You Ready For Your Appointment?

"And as it is appointed unto men, once to die but after this, the judgment: so Christ was once offered to bear the sins of many; and unto them that look for him shall he appear the second time without sin unto salvation." (Hebrews 9:27,28 KJV)

An appointment is an arrangement to meet someone in a particular time and place. It is a mutual agreement or engagement.

Each of us have an appointment that we have to keep. In the natural sense, we have appointments with doctors or lawyers, friends or acquaintances.

We get all dressed up to make our appointments. We rush out of the house, rush down the highway and then rush to make our appointments on time.

We say to our friends; I will meet you at a certain place at an appointed hour. If we cannot make our appointments, we change them or call and cancel them.

But when it comes down to our soul, we must realize that we are not going to live forever in this body and our soul has to one-day leave this body and find another home to spend eternity in.

Regardless to the time or place, this is one appointment we all have to keep. According to our reference scripture, Hebrews 9:27; all of us have an appointment with death.

Now, this is not a sad and sordid story of who will or will not go to Hell. It is an encouraging message of who will spend eternity with Jesus Christ. It is an inspirational message of hope, knowing that my soul and your soul will rest in the arms of our Savior, our Redeemer, our God and our King, forever and ever and ever.

Death is not the end of life; it is just the beginning. Apostle Paul wrote in Philippians 1:21:

"For to me, to live is Christ and to die is gain." (NIV)

So, viewing it from a spiritual standpoint, we who are born again of the seed of Christ, all have a future appointment with life and not death.

Galatians 2:20 states:

"I have been crucified with Christ and I no longer live, but Christ lives in me. The life I live in the body, I live by faith in the Son of God, who loved me and gave Himself for me." (NIV)

The life that I live in the flesh or in this body, is not the kind of life that has been divinely appointed for me.

Before the fall of mankind, they lived a life of rest and ease. A life free from pain, cares and woes. A life void of disappointments and troubles.

They lived a divinely appointed life. And now, because of the mercies of God, we who serve Jesus will be blessed to live a life of eternal bliss, joy and peace in Heaven with Him. A life we were always destined to live.

If you are somewhat as I am, you dread going to the dentist, because you know that it may involve a needle of some sort. Or you may not like keeping your doctor's appointment fearing bad news.

But believe me when I say, that this appointment with everlasting life, is one that you may want to keep. Heaven is not a made up place; it is not a pretend city, Heaven is real.

The Bible is a sacred book, II Peter 1:20,21 affirms:

"Knowing this first that no prophecy of the scriptures is of any private interpretation. For the prophecy came not in old time by the will of man, but holy men of God spake as they were moved by the Holy Spirit" (KJV)

Proverbs 30:5 declares:

"Every word of God is pure: it is a shield unto them that put their trust in Him." (KJV)

It is in the pages of this sacred book that we learn about the home of the redeemed called Heaven.

Revelation 21:18, 21,22 declares:

"The wall was made of jasper, and the city of pure gold, as pure as glass. The 12 gates were 12 pearls, each gate made of a single pearl. The great street of the city was of pure gold, like transparent glass. I did not see a temple in the city, because the Lord God Almighty and the lamb are its temple." (NIV)

"The city does not need the sun, or the moon, to shine in it: for the glory of God gives it light and the Lamb is its lamp." (NIV)

"the nations will walk by its light, and the kings of the earth will bring their splendor into it. On no day will its gates ever be shut, for there is no night there." (NIV)

Revelation 22:1,3,5 further declares:

"Then the angel showed me the river of the water of life, as clear as crystal, flowing from the throne of God and of the Lamb down the middle of the great street of the city. On each side of the river stood the tree of life, bearing 12 crops of fruit, yielding it's fruit every month. And the leaves of the tree are for the healing of the nations. No longer will there be any curse. The throne of God and of the Lamb will be in the city and his servants will serve him. There will be no more night. they will not need the light of a lamp or the light of the sun, for the Lord god will give them light. And they will reign forever and ever." (NIV)

Jesus shared many spiritual truths with his disciples that are still relevant for the church in this age.

He stated in John 14:1-3:

"Do not let your hearts be troubled. Believe in God, believe also in me. In my Father's house there are many dwelling places. If it were not so, would I have told you that I go to prepare a place for you, I will come again and will take you to myself, so that where I am, there you may be also." (NIV)

Many reserve this passage of scripture for a funeral or "home going' (as some would call it) to strengthen the hearts and ease the minds of family members and loved ones who are grieving.

Jesus, however, did not limit His message to funerals. He taught a message of peace and enlightenment, telling his disciples that there was nothing to be troubled about. There was no need for them to worry.

Yes, He was going away but only to prepare a place, (a home) for them and for those who would come to know him.

Then Jesus promised that He would return one day to take them where he was. There is nothing sad or disarming about that promise. It is a sure and determined fact that those who die in the Lord will be raised to everlasting life.

In Revelation 14:13, the aging Apostle John wrote:

"And I heard a voice from Heaven saying write this down: Blessed are those who die in the Lord from now on" "Yes" says the Spirit, they are blessed indeed, for they will rest from their hard work; for their good deeds follow them." (New Living Translation)

This means that all Christians should be encouraged during their time of testing; during their time of service and in times of need. Why? Because they will finally rest from their labor.

According to Job 3:17:

"There the wicked cease from troubling and there the weary are at rest." (English Standard Version)

It is a rest from sin, sorrow, temptation, conflict and pain. It is an everlasting rest.

II Corinthians 5:8,9 further confirms:

"Therefore we are always confident and know that as long as we are at home in the body we are away from the Lord. We are confident, I say and would prefer to be away from the body and at home with the Lord. So we make it our goal to please him, whether we are at home in the body of way from it" (NIV)

The Apostle Paul stated in II Thessalonians 4:16,17:

"For the Lord Himself will come down from Heaven, with a loud command, with the voice of the archangel and with the trumpet call of God, and the dead in Christ will rise first. After that, we who are still alive and are left will be caught up together with them in the clouds to meet the Lord in the air, and so we will be with the Lord forever." (NIV)

All of these scriptures are the reason why I am asking you today; are you ready for your appointment? Not an appointment with death but an appointment with life. Your eternal life is a package deal. When you come to Jesus, repent of your sins and confess that you have received his grace and mercy; then the future life that God is offering you becomes yours automatically.

Dear Jesus,

Give me this abundant life that you are offering and make me worthy to live forever in Heaven with you. Amen!

•

XXI

SING UNTO THE LORD
A NEW SONG

"O sing unto the Lord a new song; sing unto the Lord all the earth. Sing unto the Lord, bless His name, shew forth His salvation from day to day." (Psalms 96:1-2 KJV)

This Psalm is a song of worship and praise to God. In it, we are being exalted to show forth the holiness of God every day. King David used this Psalm when he brought the Ark of the Covenant back into Jerusalem.

They brought the Ark back and set it in the middle of the tent that David had pitched for it. When they brought the Ark in, David came in singing, dancing and shouting.

All the people joined in the sweet refrain. Michal, Saul daughter, saw her husband coming in leaping and dancing and praising God and she despised him in her heart. When David returned home, his wife said to him:

"How glorious was the king of Israel today, who uncovered himself today in the eyes of the handmaids of his servants, as one of the vain fellows shamelessly uncovereth himself!" (II Samuel 6: 20-KJV)

But David said to her: *"It was before the Lord, which chose me before thy father; and before all his house, to appoint me ruler over the people of the Lord, over Israel: therefore, will I play before the Lord." (II Samuel 6:21-KJV)*

David reminded her who he was and why he was praising God. He said that he was not doing it before men but before the Lord. David exalted all of the people to sing to the Lord; to sing a new song unto the Lord. They were to declare his glory and make his marvelous works known through all the land. Honoring God and worshipping Him in the beauty of Holiness, is was David's way of saying that the Lord is great and He is greatly to be praised.

The songs that we sing from day to day should reflect the kind of life that we live. We need to learn to let the praises of God fill our hearts every day.

Singing to the Lord is the best way to express our love and devotion to Him. It helps us to appreciate and love Him more.

Ephesians 5:19 declares:

"Speaking to yourselves in psalms and hymns and spiritual songs, singing and making melody in your heart to the Lord." (KJV)

This passage of scriptures encourages us to do 2 things:

1. **Speak to yourself in psalms, hymns and spiritual songs.**
   Have you ever spoken to yourself in a song? We are faced with trials daily and it is through the words of a Psalm, hymn or spiritual song that we find strength to continue on the paths of righteousness. While in the middle of a storm, I heard the words of this song on the radio as I was driving along. The songstress said:

   "Don't let the problems get you down. Don't let the situation make you frown. Don't let the hard times get the best of you. Hold your head up and walk on through. I know it's hard to see your way. The devil throwing darkness all in your way. Don't thrown in the towel, stay in the fight. Jesus will be there. He is the way, the truth and the light and everything will be alright."

All of a sudden, I found the strength that I was in so desperate need of and I spoke to myself in the words of that songs saying, Yes! Everything WILL be alright.

How often do we listen to music and never hear the words? How is it that we can move to the rhythm of the song and never quite get the message? But my friends, I encourage you today to hear the words, receive the message and lift up your head.

2. **Sing and make melody in your heart to the Lord.**
   We need to stop singing the same old boring song. Stop singing a song of defeat, a song of doubt and despair. We need to stop singing songs that convey negative meanings and bring a sense of hopelessness to our souls. No, we need to sing and make a melody in our hearts to the Lord. If you feel that your voice was not meant for singing, then be sure to carry a melody in your heart. Singing blesses God and it blesses us too. Reference is made to singing over 100 times in the Bible. That means that singing is very important to God.

But what are we to sing?

First, of all, the scripture tells us to sing Psalms.

The Psalms were Israel's hymnbook. They sang songs of confidence, songs of thanksgiving, songs of praise, songs of deliverance and songs about their Messiah. "the Hebrew title for the Book of Psalms is "tehilim", meaning "praises". If one word could be chosen to describe the book, certainly "praises" would qualify, for there is no Psalm that does not contain an element of praise." (King James Study Bible note p. 857)

Second, we are to sing hymns:

A lot of hymns have been forgotten today. Hymns such as: *"what a friend we have in Jesus, all our sins and griefs to bear. What a privilege it is to carry, everything to God in prayer."* Or hymns such as: *Amazing Grace how sweet the sound, that saved a wretch like me. I once was lost but now, I'm found. I was blind, but now I see.*

How can we forget such melodious hymns such as?

"I heard the voice of Jesus say, come unto me and rest. Lay down, thou weary one lay down, thy head upon my breast"

Or *"there is a fountain filled with blood, drawn from Emmanuel's veins. And sinners plunge beneath that flow, lose all their guilty stains."*

These hymns carried with them a reality of the soul's pilgrimage here on earth. We can never escape their message and should never forget to fill our hearts with the hymns of old.

Thirdly, we are to sing Spiritual songs:

Spirituals, as they are so often called, carry a deep, deep meaning. Spirituals uplift the soul and makes the heart glad. The Negro slaves were in bondage but their spirits were free. The spirituals they sang were not just any ordinary songs; they had a hidden meaning.

For example, the song "Steal away home" told them which route to take to freedom.

The song "Wade in the water" told them to travel along the rivers so that the dogs would not pick up their scent.

The song, "In that great getting up morning, fare ye well" spoke about the escape to freedom and if the slave traders happen to catch them and kill them; they knew that one day they would get up out of the grave and to this old life, they said "fare ye well".

Then there are instrumental songs that help the believer to testify of the goodness of God. In I Samuel 16:23 we read:

"And it came to pass when the evil spirit from God came upon Saul, that David took an harp and played with his hand, so Saul was refreshed and was well and the evil spirit departed from him" (KJV)

If you want the enemy to flee, play some nice, soft, instrumental music that is able to soothe the soul and refresh the spirit. The Bible records in II Samuel 6:5, that David and all the house of Israel played all types of instruments such as: harps, psalteries (another type of a harp such as a lyre), timbels (similar to the modern tambourine), cymbals and cornets (a brass instrument resembling a trumpet).

Instrumental music has very little words, if any, and creates an air of worship and reverence. There are many times in our lives in which words are not needed.

Romans 8:26 affirms:

"Likewise the Spirit helps us in our weakness. For we do not know what to pray for as we ought, but the Spirit himself intercedes for us with groaning too deep for words. (English Standard Version)

Today, we have Gospel music. It has been said that Gospel music is so powerful, that it reaches beyond the barriers of race, creed or color. Songs like: "How Great Thou art" or "I get joy when I think about what he has done for me". Songs like, "Glory, glory, Hallelujah, since I laid my burdens down" and "Can't nobody do me like Jesus". One of my personal favorites is "When we all get to heaven, what a day of rejoicing that will be, when we all see Jesus, we will sing and shout the victory".

Psalm 137 tells the story of the Israelites who had lost their song. Verses 1-4 declares:

"By the rivers of Babylon, there we sat down, yea, we wept, when we remembered Zion. We hanged our harps upon the willows in the midst thereof; For there they that carried us away captive required of us a song and they that wasted us required of us mirth, saying, sing us one

of those songs of Zion. How shall we sing the Lord's song in a strange land?" (KJV)

You see, the Israelites had been taken into bondage because of their disobedience to God. By the rivers of Babylon, they had been persecuted. They had been beaten and they suffered major hardship. So there by the rivers they sat down. What a picture of deep despair and desperation. There they sat down and there they wept.

The Israelites are not there because they want to be. They are there because their city has been destroyed. They are there because the Babylonians have taken them captive and put them on slave labor. These people are down there on the banks of the river of Babylon because they have sinned against God. And now, they have no heart for singing. Have you ever been in that predicament?

The people are down by the rivers of Babylon weeping, wailing and crying, instead of singing. Not only that but they have put down the instruments of music. They have lost their heart for singing and have lost all desire to even play an instrumental song. They hung their harps on the willow tree as a sign that they had given up on life, itself.

The people of Babylon had heard about the singing in Israel. They heard how the Israelites praised and blessed their God. Israel was world famous for their worship and their music. King David had set in order, singers and musicians who ministered before the Lord in the tabernacle. When Solomon had finished building the Temple, they all took their respective places to minister before the Lord continually. They bowed down with their faces to the ground and they worshipped and praised God for all that He had done until the glory of the Lord filled the entire house where they were. (II Chronicles 7).

During the festival season, the people would gather around and sing songs. It is estimated that over 100,000 people gathered in and around the temple, singing praises to God. Can you imagine what a glorious sound that was to God? To hear all those voices blending together to create a harmonious rendition of music.

But now the Temple was burned. Jerusalem lay in ruins and the people are doing slave labor.

The Babylonians said to them: *"sing us one of those songs of Zion."*

But the Israelites replied: **"how** *can we sing the Lord's song in a strange* *land?*

They had lost their song. Years before his, the Israelites had come out of Egypt with singing and dancing. They crossed the Red Sea and they sang songs. They reached the Promised land and they sang songs. The Levites carrying the Ark of the Covenant were singing. The tribe of Judah came behind with singing and praise unto the Lord. But now, there was no singing, no mirth, no laughter and no music. They felt a spirit of hopelessness and despair. It is yet true today, that how we feel spiritually has a lot to do with what type of music we sing or whether or not we sing at all. But let us take heed to the words of the Psalmists who wrote:

"Make a joyful noise unto the Lord, all ye lands. Serve the Lord with gladness; come before his presence with singing." (Psalm 100:1-2-KJV)

"O clap your hands all ye people; shout unto God with the voice of triumph. Sing praises to God, sing praises; sing praises unto our King, sing praises" (Psalm 47:1,6-KJV)

"Sing aloud unto God our strength, make a joyful noise unto the God of Jacob. Take a psalm, bring the timbel, bring the harp and blow the trumpet." (Psalm 81:1-3-KJV)

"I will sing, yea, I will sing praises unto the Lord." (Psalm 27:6-KJV)

"O come let us sing unto the Lord. Let us make a joyful noise to the rock of our salvation. Let us come before his presence with thanksgiving and make a joyful noise unto him with psalms." (Psalm 95:1-2-KJV)

"Praise ye the Lord, how good it is to sing praises to our God. How pleasant and fitting to praise him." (Psalm 147:1-NIV)

"Let the saints rejoice in this honor and sing for joy on their beds."(Psalm 149: 5-NIV)

This book cannot contain all of the references made to music, singing, worshipping and praising given to us in God's Word. I can only attempt to convey to you the importance of singing and worship. As I write, my heart is filled with melodies that cannot be expressed in words alone. But I exalt you today to take time to render a spontaneous selection of music to God the Father. He will be greatly pleased. Hallelujah!

Dear Father,

Forgive us for neglecting to honor you through the gifts of music that you have given to us. Help us to realize how important and necessary are the songs which we so easily take for granted. Let us be mindful of the words contained in a hymn or song of praise and help us to live by those precious lyrics. In Jesus' name we pray. Amen!

XXII

MY HEART BELONGS TO YOU LORD

"A new heart also will I give you and a new spirit will I put within you and I will take away the stony heart out of your flesh and I will give you a heart of flesh" (Ezekiel 36:26-KJV)

When the Bible talks about the heart of man, it is speaking about the seat of man's emotions, the very core of man's existence, the soul.

Time after time, we have given our heart to one thing or another or to one person or another. Many times, in giving our hearts away, our hearts have been broken and bruised, simply because we made a wrong decision. We made a decision with our emotions. We made a decision when we were angry and hurt. Some of us made decisions based on a moment of pleasure.

We quickly made many decisions at the last minute. We realize later that most of them were wrong decisions. Then again, we could have made a right decision but the execution of that decision was wrong and we did not follow through with what God had placed in our spirits.

In Deuteronomy 13:1-4, God spoke to the Israelites stating:

"If there arise among you a prophet or a dreamer of dreams and giveth thee a sign or a wonder, And the sign or the wonder come to pass, whereof he spake unto thee, saying, let us go after other gods, which thou hast not known, and let us serve them. Thou shalt not hearken unto the words of that prophet, or that dreamer of dreams; for the Lord

your God proveth you, to know whether ye love the Lord your God with all your heart and with all your soul. Ye shall walk after the Lord your God, and fear him, and keep his commandments, and obey his voice, and ye shall serve him, and cleave unto him." (KJV)

God told his people that if anyone, regardless to who it was, dreams a dream or sees a vision, telling them to go after other gods, that they are not to listen to that prophet or dreamer. That sign is telling them to forsake the Lord, change course and change their direction, and they are not to take heed to it.

God spoke to His people by visions, signs and the prophets, so their only means of communicating with God had to be through a prophet. Unfortunately, there were many dreamers in Israel and there were countless prophets, some true and some false.

The prophets that Israel trusted in, broke God's covenant and began to follow after other gods; that is why God warned them not to give their heart away to just anybody. God was testing them, to see if they would love Him, only, with all of their heart and soul.

The enemy will make it appear as if God has forsaken us. He will put blinders on our eyes so that we will believer that God is not answering our prayers; but through all our frustrations, my friends, we must not give our hearts away.

In psalms 51:10, David cried out to the Lord. He said:

"create in me a clean heart, O God, and renew a right spirit within me."

David knew that his heart had been wandering. His heart was looking for love in all the wrong places. His spirit man was craving for things that could not satisfy, nor profit him spiritually. So he cried out to God saying, wash me, cleanse me, purge me and restore me. Create in me a clean heart.

That should be our cry today. Lord, cleanse my heart. Lord, wash my mind. Lord purge me through and through.

Concerning a washing, the Apostle Peter said to Jesus in St. John 13:8:

"Thou shalt never wash my feet. Jesus answered him, If I wash thee not, thou hast no part with me. "(KJV)

Peter then replied: *"Lord, not my feet only, but also my hands and my head." John 13:9 (KJV)*

Peter was requesting a thorough cleansing. He did not want to give his heart away. But yet, we know that we can have the best of intentions and still miss the mark as Peter did later on when Jesus was taken by the soldiers.

In II Chronicles 26, we read about a king named Uzziel. Uzziel was 16 years old when he became king. He did what was right in the sight of the Lord. He sought after God with all of his heart. The Bible says that as long as he sought the Lord, God caused him to prosper.

God helped Uzziel against the Philistines and the Ammonites. His name spread across the land, all the way to the borders of Egypt. Uzziel had a host of fighting men numbering 307,500. He made helmets, shield, bows and arrows, slings to cast stones and towers to shoot arrows. He built fortified cities and dug wells. He had cattle and vineyards in abundance. God helped Uzziel until he was strong, so strong that no one could stand against him.

Then verse 16 reads:

"but when he was strong, his heart was lifted up to his destruction." (KJV)

He went into the sanctuary of God to burn incense to God. This was forbidden for kings to do, only the priests of God were to burn incense to God. When the priests told King Uzziel that it was unlawful for him to burn incense, he persisted in his wrong doing. As he lifted the censer to burn incense, God struck him with leprosy. King Uzziel was a leper until the day of his death. He was cut off from God and from the people of God. Why? Because he gave his heart away.

In our reference scripture, God spoke to Ezekiel and told him that the people needed a new heart. God, Himself would provide this heart. He would give them a new heart and a new spirit as well. He would take the stony heart out and replace it with a heart of flesh. The new heart would be soft and pliable. It would be a heart that strives to please and serve God. It would be a heart that says, I belong to you Lord.

Many heart conditions, naturally speaking, can cause the heart to beat ill-regularly. Blocked blood vessels can lead to heart failure or a heart attack. Other conditions affect the muscles of the heart that can cause chest pain or a stroke. Yet, many of these symptoms could have been prevented or treated with smart lifestyle choices such as exercise, diet and proper heath care. (www.mayoclinic.org)

In Proverbs 4:23, we are admonished to:

"keep thy heart with all diligence for out of it are the issues of life."
(KJV)

"above all else, guard your heart, for everything you do flows from it"
(NIV)

"guard your heart above all else, for it determines the course of your life." (NLT)

"Is not this a plain allusion to the arteries which carry the blood from the heart through the whole body, and to the utmost extremities? As long as the heart is capable of receiving and propelling the blood, so long life is continued. Now as the heart is the fountain whence all the streams of life proceed, care must be taken that the fountain be not stopped us nor injured. A double watch for its safety must be kept up. So in spiritual things: the heart is the seat of the Lord of life and glory; and the streams of spiritual life proceed from him to all the

powers and faculties of the soul. Watch with all diligence, that this fountain be not sealed up, nor these streams of life be cut off." (Clark's Commentary on the Bible.)

What more can I add? Only that there are uninvited guests who struggle to take possession of our hearts. We must guard the heart with all that is within us and be on the lookout for all unwanted visitors. Pride is one of those visitors that we must guard against. So is, malice, evil thoughts, wickedness, deceit, foolishness, covetousness and blasphemy. According to Mark 7:23: "all these evil things come from within, and defile the man." (KJV)

For it is from within, from the human heart that all of these things come. Our hearts belong to Jesus Christ. That is why we are told to purify the heart, to sanctify the heart, to sing and make melody in the heart and to draw near to God with a pure heart.

That is why we are encouraged to:

"Let the peace of Christ be in control in your heart (for you were in face called as one body to this peace), and be thankful." (Colossians 3:15-NET Bible)

Dear Father,

Help me to let your Word dwell in me that I may allow your peace to keep my heart, both naturally and spiritually. Amen!

XXIII

WHO SHALL ROLL THE STONE AWAY?

"And when the Sabbath was past, Mary Magdalene, and Mary the mother of James, and Salome, had brought sweet spices, that they might come and anoint him. And very early in the morning the first day of the week, they came unto the sepulcher at the rising of the sun. And they said among themselves, who shall roll us away the stone from the door of the sepulcher? And when they looked, they saw that the stone was rolled away; for it was very great." (KJV)

In reading these verses of scripture, we conclude that the Sabbath had ended at sundown. Jesus had been crucified and buried and the women came to anoint his body. The same women who were at the cross, were now at the tomb.

The disciples had the attitude that since Jesus was dead, it would be better for them if they stayed undercover until all the excitement about his death had passed. They felt that if they remained in hiding and out of sight long enough that maybe no one would connect them with the Messiah. It seems as though none of them intended to go to the tomb.

But our scripture text informs us that it was very early in the morning when the women brought spices to anoint the body of Jesus. They were faced with the difficulty, however, of moving the stone from the door of the tomb and they said among themselves—who shall roll the stone away from the door of the sepulcher? (v.3)

That is the question I ask you today. who shall roll the stone away?

According to Biblical history, stones were used for several things:

- For punishment
- To mark the grave of a notorious person
- To build altars of worship
- To signify holy things

It is not my aim to dwell on any of these meanings. I endeavor, I wonder, I ponder and I speculate about the stones that are upon the hearts of men. Who will take that stone away?

Ecclesiastes 3:1-5 states:

"To everything there is a season, and a time to every purpose under the heaven: a time to be born, and a time to die; a time to plant and a time to pluck up that which is planted; a time to kill and a time to heal; a time to break down and a time to build up; a time to weep and a time to laugh; a time to mourn and a time to dance; a time to cast away stones and a time to gather stones together; a time to embrace and a time to refrain from embracing."(KJV)

It has always been and is yet now the time to cast away stones, especially the stones that clutter the hearts of men and keep them from receiving the glorious message of the Gospel.

There are all types of stones:

- Stones that keep us from reaching out to an awesome and marvelous God
- Stones that people throw at us to destroy and punish us
- Stones of all shapes and sizes
- Stones that bruise and hurt

- Stones that accuse and abuse
- Stones which block us from entering the kingdom of God

Matthew 13:3-6 declares: ***"Behold, a sower went forth to sow; and when he sowed, some seeds fell by the wayside and the fowls came and devoured them up: some fell on stony places, where they had not much earth: and forthwith they sprung up, because they had no deepness of earth: and when the sun was up, they were scorched; and because they had no root, they withered away. (KJV)***

Then in verses 18 through 23, Jesus explains to his disciples the meaning of the parable.

- The seed depicts the Word of God
- The sower is the preacher, teacher, evangelist or whoever gives out the Word of God.
- The wayside is the path through the field, there the Word falls but is trampled upon by men and eaten up by the fowls of the air.
- Then there are the stony places. The seed falls between the cracks and quickly springs up but because there is not adequate root-age or moisture, the seed is scorched by the sun and thereby withers away.

There are millions of individuals who hear the Word of God and believe it but because of the stones that are upon their hearts, they refuse to receive it.

Just like the women at the tomb; they come to a hard place in life and asks themselves-Who is going to help me to get rid of this stone?

- The stones of doubt and failure
- The stones of rejection and self-pity

Who is going to help me roll those stones away from my heart that I may experience the fullness of joy that knowing Jesus brings?

The women who went to the tomb knew that the stone was there but they acted in faith and went to the grave anyway. They were on a mission to make sure that Jesus' body was properly anointed. God always makes a way when we step out in faith.

Ezekiel 36:26 tells us that God has promised that He will take away that stone. It declares:

"A new heart also will I give you, and a new spirit will I put within you: and I will take away the stony heart out of your flesh, and I will give you a heart of flesh." (KJV)

Jesus was crucified to give us a new heart.

Isaiah 53:3-5 affirms:

"He is despised and rejected of men, a man of sorrows and acquainted with grief: and we hid as it were our faces from him; he was despised and we esteemed him not.

Surely he hath borne our griefs and carried our sorrows yet we did esteem him stricken, smitten of God, and afflicted.

But he was wounded for our transgressions, he was bruised for our iniquities: the chastisement of our peace was upon him and with his stripes we are healed."(KJV)

All of these things were done to Jesus for our benefit.

- He was despised---to disdain or scorn
- Rejected ---abandoned
- Man of sorrows—severe pain
- Acquainted with grief---injuries, severe personal suffering
- Stricken-- hit, stuck
- Smitten—stuck down, afflicted
- Afflicted—troubled, burdened, distress
- Wounded—hurt, harmed, injured, scarred or damaged
- Yet he bore our griefs—our spiritual sickness, our stony hearts, our rebellion, our stubbornness

He was stricken, smitten and afflicted. He was wounded that we might be healed. Our hearts and bodies needed healing. We needed forgiveness and Jesus made it possible that we could receive spiritual healing from God the Father.

Jesus rolled that stone away for us. Now it is up to us to come out of that grave of doom, gloom and spiritual darkness.

You see, you cannot roll that stone away by yourself because it is too heavy. That sin is too heavy. That problems weights too much. You cannot carry that burden. All of your problems are weights. Worry is a weight. Complaining is a weight. Doubt is a weight. The women could not have rolled the stone away from the door of the tomb because it represented the sins of the whole world. Neither can you roll the stone away from your heart. You need help.

The Bible says that when the women reached the tomb, they found that an angel had rolled the stone away and that Jesus was no longer there.

The tomb was empty. The fact of the empty tomb tells us that God provided a way of escape for us. He has taken the stone out of the way and now he is sitting on it. The enemy cannot put the stone back. He can bind us no longer. He cannot keep us in sin any longer. Jesus has set us free. He rolled the stone away. Don't keep the stone at the door, Jesus has already taken it away for you. Receive him and be set free. Hallelujah!

Thank You Jesus for taking my burdens, my worries and afflictions to the cross. Thank you for taking that heavy stone away.

XXIV

WHAT WILL WE DO WITH GOD'S DIVINE GIFTS

"And Solomon loved the Lord, walking in the statues of David his father; only he sacrificed and burnt incense in high places.

And the king went to Gibeon to sacrifice there; for that was the great high place: a thousand burnt offerings did Solomon offer upon that altar.

In Gibeon the Lord appeared to Solomon in a dream by night: and God said, ask what I shall give thee.

And Solomon said, thou hast showed unto thy servant David my father great mercy, according as he walked before thee in truth, and in righteousness, and in uprightness of heart with thee. And thou hast kept for him this great kindness, that thou hast given him a son to sit on his throne, as it is this day.

And now, O Lord God, thou hast made thy servant king instead of David my father: and I am but a little child: I know not how to go out or come in.

And thy servant is in the midst of thy people which thou hast chosen, a great people, that cannot be numbered nor counted for multitude.

Give therefore thy servant an understanding heart to judge thy people, that I may discern between good and bad: for who is able to judge this so great a people?

And the speech pleased the Lord, that Solomon had asked this thing.

And God said unto him, because thou hast asked this thing, and hast not asked for thyself long life; neither hast asked riches for thyself, not hast asked the life of thine enemies; but hast asked for thyself understanding to discern judgment.

Behold I have done according to thy words: lo, I have given thee a wise and understanding heart; so that there is none like thee before thee, neither after thee shall any rise like unto thee.

And I have also given thee that which thou hast not asked, both riches, and honor; so that there shall not be any among the kings like unto thee all thy days.

And if thou wilt walk in my ways, to keep my statues and my commandments, as thy father David did walk, then I will lengthen thy days." (I Kings 3:3-14--KJV)

What will we do with God's divine gifts?

If we had one request, what would we ask for?

Will our request please God?

Will we receive all of God's goodness, then turn from him?

These are the question, and many more, that we have to ponder as we review a few episodes in the life of Israel's wisest king, Solomon.

According to our reference scripture, Solomon loved the Lord with all of his heart, and he walked in the way of his father David, Israel's greatest king. While in Gibeon, offering sacrifices, God appeared to him in a dream and God said to Solomon *"ask what I shall give thee?"*

Solomon's reply was: *"give therefore thy servant, an understanding heart, that I may discern between good and bad."*

And verse 10 tells us that the speech pleased the Lord.

Solomon began his reign in faith and with love for God. He asked for a most special gift and God granted his request. However, God's gift was no guarantee that Solomon would always persist in doing what the Lord wanted him to do. For this reason, God told Solomon, that if he would walk in His ways as his father David did, that God, Himself would give Solomon, a long and prosperous life.

Solomon called himself- "God's servant", thereby indicating his desire to submit willingly to God's service. Solomon knew that God loved him. He understood that he was in God's hands as clay. Solomon realized that it was God who had anointed him to be king over His people. When Solomon spoke in faith, calling himself God's servant, he understood the full implications of what this meant. It meant that Solomon's first desire was to please God.

We have established that Solomon was committed to God in service, wanting only to be His servant. Now let us consider Solomon's request:

"give therefore thy servant an understanding heart to judge thy people, that I may discern between good and bad: for who is ble to judge this so great a people?"

When Solomon asked God for an "understanding heart", he was asking God to help him to give very close attention to details and to make the right decisions concerning the Israelite people. Decisions that could be felt way down deep on the inside as being the right or the best thing to do (a little something that we call unction).

So in short Solomon was saying, that his desire is to pay close attention to that which is right, best and pleasing to God, in contrast to that which is worthless, wicked or destructive. He wanted to know in his heart of hearts that he had made the right decision for everyone involved.

Solomon's request was a very powerful one. That is why God was so pleased with it and why God so graciously granted him much more than what he asked for.

Solomon proved that he was truly and divinely gifted by God by the first incident we see him dealing with recorded in I Kings 3:16-28.

This situation dealt with 2 women who were harlots, living together in the same house. Both of them gave birth to baby boys, one of whom died during the night due to suffocation. The one whose child died, got up at midnight, after realizing that her child had died, took the living child from the other mother and placed her dead child in the other mother's arms.

When the other mother awoke in the morning, she knew that the child that was in her arms was not her child. She questioned the other mother who claimed that the living child was indeed hers. When the matter could not be resolved, they took the dispute to King Solomon.

Both mothers came to Solomon claiming to have given birth to the living child and not the dead child.

Solomon heard the dispute and responded in wisdom by saying: ***"bring me a sword...divide the living child in two and give half to one and half to the other." (vv. 24,25)***

The mother of the living child immediately spoke up saying: ***"give her the living child, in no wise slay it." (v. 26)***

But the other mother said: ***"Let it be neither mine not thine, but divide it." (v. 26)***

Then Solomon discerned who the real mother was because he paid attention to the details of the story, the reaction of both mothers and the compassion and cries of the genuine mother.

Verse 28 states: ***"all Israel heard of the judgment which the king had judged and they feared the king; for they saw that the wisdom of God was in him, to do judgment." (KJV)***

What did Solomon do with God's divine gifts?

According to I Kings 4:30,31: ***"Solomon's wisdom excelled the wisdom of all the children of the east country and all the wisdom of Egypt. For he was wiser than all men." (KJV)***

Verse 34 states: ***"And there came of all people to hear the wisdom of Solomon, from all kings of the earth, which had heard of his wisdom." (KJV)***

Solomon put his gift to great use, being wiser and richer than any other king. But toward the end of his life, Solomon misused and abused the favor with which God had so graciously blessed him.

He showed much wisdom in all that he attempted to do, except in his love of many strange women; this brought about his downfall.

He started out in sincerity, as many of God's children do, but in his zest to acquire material things, Solomon neglected his spiritual life and relationship with God.

Throughout his life, Solomon remembered what God had promised him that faithful night, "riches and honor". But instead of allowing God to fulfill His promises, Solomon went about to establish his own riches and his own righteousness.

In Ecclesiastes 2:4-10: Solomon stated;

"I made me great works; I build me houses; I planted me vineyards;

I made me gardens and orchards, and I planted trees in them of all kind of fruits:

I made me pools of water to water therewith the wood that bringeth forth trees:

I got me servants and maidens, and had servants born in my house, also I had great possessions of great and small cattle above all that were in Jerusalem before me;

I gathered me also silver and gold, and the peculiar treasure of kings and of the provinces: I got me men singers and women singers, and the delights of sons of men, as musical instruments and that of all sorts.

So I was great and increased more than all that were before me in Jerusalem; also my wisdom remained with me.

And whatsoever mine eye desired I kept not from them, I withheld not my heart from any joy; for my heart rejoiced in all my labor; and this was my portion of all my labor." (KJV)

Leaving God completely out of the picture, Solomon glorified himself as some sort of a god. He stated: **I DID THIS AND I DID THAT, I MADE THIS AND I MADE THAT, I GOT THIS AND I GOT THAT. I PLANTED THIS AND I BUILT THAT. I WAS GREAT AND I WAS RICH. I WAS WISE AND I REJOICED IN MY LABOR AND MY PORTION.**

All of his self-righteousness and selfish desires stripped and crippled this once humble servant of God and it would take a miraculous intervention to unveil that true, genuine and loving servant, that he was before.

Now, to use the famous words of Solomon, *"let us hear the conclusion of the whole matter"*

In Ecclesiastes 12:13-14, we find Solomon at the end of a life, which he called vanity, saying:

"Let us hear the conclusion of the whole matter: Fear God and keep his commandments; for this is the whole duty of man. For God shall bring every work into judgment, with every secret thing, whether it be good, or whether it be evil." (KJV)

THERE HE IS! That humble servant he started out to as.

THERE HE IS! That wise king God made him to be.

Let us learn from his life but always remember the conclusion. Like Solomon, we should ask in faith, believing God will answer.

Like Solomon, we should use our God-given gifts to their full potential.

Unlike Solomon, however, we should never turn from following the one who gave us the gift.

What are we going to do with the divine gift that God gave us? Here is what we should do:

In II Timothy 1:6 Paul told Timothy to:

- *"stir up the gift of God" (KJV)*
- *"Afresh the gift of God" (NASB)*
- *"keep ablaze the gift of God (Holman Christian Standard Bible)*
- *" fan into flames the gift of God' (ISV)*

Regardless to the words used or to which translation we follow, our job is to keep the gift of God alive in us.

Dear God, thank you for your divine gifts that you have given to me, may I always cherish them and use them for your glory. In Jesus name I pray. Amen!

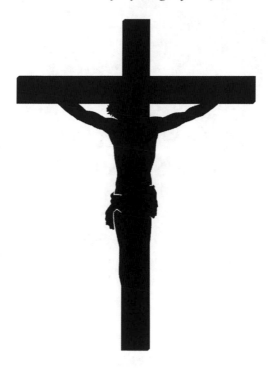

•

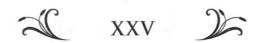 XXV

GOD IS SPEAKING, ARE WE LISTENING?

God our Father, hears our hearts cry. He understands the anxieties which we face from day to day. He listens to our complaints, our groaning and our prayers. Yes! He is there for us.

We can all agree that we serve an awesome God who hears and answers prayer, even the very faintest of cries.

But the question today is not--does God hear me? But it is--do I hear God? Am I listening to God? God is speaking to us, are we listening?

We hear a lot of things from minute to minute, hour to hour and day to day. We hear the cries of infants, wanting to be fed, a dry diaper or just the loving arms of its parents.

We hear the sound of birds chirping in the sky, bees buzzing over our heads and the wind rushing through the trees.

We hear about good news and most definitely, we hear about bad news.

We hear music, some soft, some sweet and some loud and overwhelming.

There are many things that demand our attention, some to our pleasure and others things not so much for our benefit. But through all of our struggles and through all of our cares and woes, can we hear the voice of the Lord?

In our reference Scripture, we read about how God spoke to Elijah the prophet, while he was on the mountain in a cave. At Elijah's lowest moment, God showed up and began to talk to him.

I Kings 19:9-13 declares:

"And he came thither unto a cave, and lodged there and behold, the word of the Lord came to him and said unto him, What doest thou here Elijah?

And he said, I have been very jealous for the Lord God of Hosts: for the children of Israel have forsaken thy covenant, thrown down thine altars and slain thy prophets with the sword: and, I, even I only, am left, and they seek my life, to take it away.

And he said, go forth and stand upon the mount before the Lord. And, behold, the Lord passed by, and a great and strong wind rent the mountains, and brake in pieces the rocks before the Lord; but the Lord was not in the wind: and after the wind an earthquake; but the Lord was not in the earthquake.

And after the earthquake a fire; but the Lord was not in the fire, and after the fire, a still small voice.

And it was so, when Elijah heard it, that he wrapped his face in his mantle and went out, and stood in the entering in of the cave and behold, there came a voice unto him and said, what doest thou here Elijah?" (KJV)

According to the Book of Kings, the prophet Elijah had spoken to the wicked King Ahab and his wife, the notorious Jezebel.

Elijah told Ahab, in I Kings 17;1--*"as the Lord God of Israel liveth, before whom I stand, there shall not be dew, nor rain these years, but according to my word."(KJV)*

Elijah had literally pronounced doom on the house of Ahab, and by his sure word of prophecy, it did not rain for 3 years.

Ahab was furious with Elijah. So furious, that toward the end of the 3 years, he called Obadiah, the governor of his house, demanding that he find Elijah and bring him to stand before the king.

Elijah on the other hand, was busy doing what the Lord had commissioned for him to do. In Zerephath, Elijah was at the home of a widow woman. The woman had one son and both of them were on the verge of starvation. (I Kings 17). The widow had a hand full of meal and only a small jar of oil. She was going to use the meal and the oil to make the last meal that her and her son would eat. Elijah asked her to make one for him first. As she obeyed the man of God, he said to her: *"...thus saith the Lord God of Israel, the barrel of meal shall not waste, neither shall the cruse of oil fail, until the day that the Lord sendeth rain upon the earth." (v.14—KJV)*

By the word of the man of God, the widow and her son survived the drought.

While Elijah was there with the widow woman, her son fell sick to the point of death. Elijah cried out to God to heal the child and restore his life. The Lord heard the prayer of Elijah and the widow received her son alive again.

After that, the Lord told Elijah to return to Ahab and tell him that it was going to rain, but Ahab had already sent out soldiers to find Elijah. As they searched for Elijah, throughout the whole land of Samaria, Ahab went in one direction and Obadiah in another.

Obadiah was a man who feared God and he knew that Elijah was a true prophet of God. When he met Elijah on the road, he fell down on his

"Powerful Words, Thoughts and Inspirations for the Soul"

face and asked him: *"is it really you, my Lord Elijah (v.7—NIV)* Elijah answered --- *"yes…go tell your master, Elijah is here. (v.8—NIV)*

Obadiah said*: "what have I done wrong, that you are handing your servant over to Ahab to be put to death…there is not a nation or kingdom where my master has not sent someone to look for you…I don't know where the Spirit of the Lord may carry you when I leave you. If I go and tell Ahab and he doesn't find you, he will kill me (v.9-13—NIV)*

Elijah then reassured Obadiah that he would present himself to Ahab that day. When Ahab saw Elijah, he immediately threw out insults and accusations saying: *"is that you, you troubler of Israel? (V.16-NIV)*

Elijah quickly answered*, "I have not made trouble for Israel, but you and your father's family have. (v.18-NIV)*

Immediately following all of this, was the contest on Mt. Carmel between Elijah (the prophet of God) and 450 prophets of Baal.

The outcome was miraculous. God sent down fire from heaven to consume the burnt sacrifices while the prophets of Baal called on Baal from morning to night to no avail. It all ended with the 450 prophets of Baal slaughtered.

All of a sudden, the sky grew dark, the clouds became heavy and the rain began to pour down upon the chariot of Ahab. Elijah wrapped his mantle around himself and ran ahead of Ahab's chariot all the way to Jezreel.

Upon hearing about the death of her prophets, Jezebel threatened Elijah's life. Fearing for his life, Elijah ran and hid himself in a cave.

It was there in that solemn, solitary place that God began to speak to his weary, worn out prophet. God speaks and Elijah hears. God askes a legitimate question: what are you doing here Elijah?

Elijah's response was a defensive one. He began explaining what he had done for God, how he was zealous for God, how he obeyed the command

151

of God and now, they were seeking his life to take it away. Elijah obviously, did not hear the question. He was not listening to God. God did not ask him—what have you done for me? God did not say—can you list for me all of your accomplishments? Did you keep track of the many prophets that Queen Jezebel killed?

No! God asked—what are YOU doing here? Figuratively speaking, God said to him: Look around you, there is so much more work to do and you my zealous, anxious prophet are here in a cave hiding. Do I need to repeat the question? Did you hear me the first time? The question was—what are you doing here?

Then God says to Elijah—*"go back the way you came" (19:15-NIV)*

Proverbs 14:12 declares: *"there is a way which seems right unto a man, but in the end it leads to death" (NIV)*

God is speaking to us as he spoke to Elijah and we must listen to him.

Figuratively speaking, God tells us—I have another way and this way leads to life everlasting. But you see, there is a problem with this way, well it's a little narrow. Sometimes there are traps on this road. You may have to cry while traveling on this road. You may even have to walk this road alone, for there are not many friends on this road. Sometimes even your family won't travel this road with you, but listen to me, that's the right way to go. The way that you are on is the crowded way. There are lots of people going that way and it looks like it's the right way to go, but it's not. That way is wide open but it only leads to death and destruction.

The GPS system in our cars tell us---in a ½ mile make a slight right turn. When we miss that turn, it says, make a U-turn if possible, your destination is straight ahead on the right.

For our own reasons, we pay close attention to the GPS system. We turn when it says turn. We stop when it says stop. We turn around when it says turn around. But how many of us are listening to God as we should?

God is saying the same thing to us as that GPS system says. You are going the wrong way, stop, turn around, go back. Do you remember that sign back there? You were supposed to make a right turn there but you missed it.

God is speaking to us. We can hear His voice loud and clear. We hear Him through the preacher who so eloquently delivers God's word. We hear God through the voices of our family members, who encourage us to follow God with all of our heart, soul and mind. We hear God's voice through television evangelists, through prophets and teachers.

But the question is, are we listening?

Just like God spoke to Elijah, He is speaking to us today. He is telling us to go back. God is saying, I did not send you here, go back, to the place where I want you to be.

Many of God's people are stressed and depressed. God is speaking to you. He did not put you on that rough and rocky road. He did not cause that painful situation to happen to you. God did not send that affliction, that awful anxiety that you experienced. Get up, turn around and go back.

When God speaks to us, will we listen?

Will we hear our master's call, when he sounds it our so plainly? I ask you today, what are you going to do? Will you listen to God or will you listen to other people?

One day, I was on that wrong road headed in the wrong direction. I saw the signs but I ignored them. I heard God's voice but I did not listen. God was saying to me: I want you to shepherd my people. I want you to stand in the gap. I want you to teach my people. I want you to give my people a healing balm. I want you to be a vessel of honor for me to use.

All of the road blocks were there but I continued to go around them. All of the street signs said "stop, go back" and do the will of the Lord, but I did not take heed to them.

Sickness took control of my body, but when God delivered me, I continued on the easy road. I did not want to hurt my family. I did not want to go against the normal way of doing things, so I thought.

Trouble showed up and blocked my path but I continued to seek God for ways around it. Now that I am where God wants me to be, I am experiencing the peace that comes from being in His perfect will. Finally, I listened to God.

What are you going to do?

Dear Jesus,

Please give me the strength to follow you all the way. Open my ears that I may listen to you regardless to what I may feel or how I think. Help me not to allow anything to get in my way from doing what you want me to do. Give me the grace to hear your voice and obey. In Jesus' name, I pray. Amen!

XXVI

HE TOUCHED ME

Luke 5:12-13:

"And it came to pass, when He was in a certain city, behold a man full of leprosy; who seeing Jesus fell on his face and besought him, saying, Lord, if thou wilt, thou canst make me clean.

And He put forth his hand and touched him, saying, I will be thou clean. And immediately the leprosy departed from him." (KJV)

It's good to be touched by Jesus. We need his touch in all circumstances and in all situations. When the pressures of life seem to cave in on us, all we need is to be able to feel the Master's hand upon us and realize that He is touching us, even to the very core of our being.

A touch can mean many things. There are gentle touches of love and compassion. There are touches that bring on feelings of regret, insecurity and shame. Then there are touches that ignite a spark of peace, joy and happiness, such is the touch of the Master's hand.

When Jesus touches you, there is a feeling of emptiness and then fullness all at the same time. All of a sudden, you feel as if He has completely emptied out of you all the negativity that has controlled your life for years. But the Savior, Redeemer and Master that we serve, never leaves us void and incomplete, He turns around and then fills our hearts with joy that we cannot explain and comfort that we do not understand.

Dr. Sharon C. Cason

Yet, it's there!

A touch that's pulling at the strings of our hearts.

A touch that's playing a sweet melody that no problem, nor care nor worry in the world could ever silence.

The sweet and gentle touch of the Master's hand.

What would we do without His touch?

His touch raised the dead.

His touch opened blinded eyes.

His touch healed sick bodies.

His touch took little children up in his arms and blessed them.

He touched the disciples with His life and they turned the world upside down.

When we are truly and genuinely touched by Jesus, we will find that we are never the same again.

Isaiah 6:6-7 reads:

"then flew one of the seraphim unto me, having a live coal in his hand, which he had taken with the tongs from off the altar. And he laid it upon my mouth and said, Lo. This hath touched thy lips and thine iniquity is taken away and thy sin is purged." (KJV)

Hallelujah!

What a glorious feeling!

To have the angel of the God (Jesus Christ incarnate) to touch your lips and then burn out all iniquity, all uncleanness and sin. How marvelous it must have been to Isaiah. He realized that he was not worthy to enter into the presence of God. He could not be an honorable servant if he remained the same. So God, in his infinite wisdom, touched his lips with a live coal from the altar, signifying purity and grace.

Isaiah heard the voice of the Lord and it asked him: ***"Whom shall I send and who will go for me? (6:8-KJV)***

Immediately Isaiah answered: ***"Here am I, send me" (6:8-KJV)***

Before the touch of the Master, Isaiah felt insignificant, insecure and unworthy. He said to God, ***"Woe is me! For I am undone; because I am a man of unclean lips and I dwell in the midst of a people with unclean lips." (6:5-KJV)***

In so many words, Isaiah said, I'm defiled! I'm polluted! I'm worthless! And I live with a people who are just as worthless and unholy as I am.

Then Isaiah said—***"mine eyes have seen the King, the Lord of Hosts" (6:5-KJV)***

Isaiah realized his condition. He knew that he needed a touch from the Master's hand. He saw the weakness of his own soul and all of his legitimate confessions caused the Holy One of Israel to send an angel to touch his lips and equip him for service.

All glory be to God because He sent His Son, one day, to be the propitiation for our sins. The ugly hand of sin, guilt and shame touched the body of Jesus so that one day his righteous hands could touch our vile bodies and made them clean.

Isaiah was never the same after the touch from the Master.

Let's take a look at the man Job. Satan came to present himself before the throne of the Lord and God said to him:

"Where have you come from?" (Job 1:6-NIV)

"Satan answered the Lord, from roaming through the earth and going back and forth in it.

Then the Lord said to Satan, have you considered my servant Job? There is no one on earth like him; he is blameless and upright, a man who fears God and shuns evil."

Does Job fear God for nothing? Satan replied. Have you not put a hedge around him and his household and everything he has? You have blessed the work of his hands, so that his flocks and herds are spread throughout the land. But stretch out your hand and strike everything he has, and he will surely curse you to your face.

The Lord said to Satan, very well, then, everything he has is in your hands, but on the man himself do not lay a finger. (Job. 1:7-12—NIV)

Job came through the first test with flying colors saying:

"Naked I came from my mother's womb and naked I will depart. The Lord gave and the Lord has taken away. May the name of the Lord be praised." (Job. 1:21—NIV)

Satan does not give up that easily, however, there was another day that he came before the throne of God and God said to him:

Job *"still maintains his integrity, though you have incited me against him to ruin him without reason."*

"Skin for skin, Satan replied. A man will give all he has for his own life. But stretch out your hand and strike his flesh and bones and he will surely curse you to your face."

"The Lord said to Satan, very well, then he is in your hands; but you must spare his life."

So Satan went out from the presence of the Lord and afflicted Job with painful sores from the soles of his feet to the top of his head." (Job. 2:3-7—NIV)

You see, Job was touched by Satan and whatever Satan touches, he destroys. Job's body was so afflicted that he sat in the ashes and scratched himself from morning until evening. But in all of this, Job declared; *"I know that my Redeemer lives and that in the end he will stand upon the earth. And after my skin has been destroyed, yet in my flesh, I will see God. (Job 19:25-26—NIV)*

Job was waiting on a touch from the Master's hand and when he received that touch, his body was restored and made whole again.

All it takes is one touch. One miraculous touch. One tremendous touch. One awesome touch from the hand of the Master.

Now, let's take a look at the Prophet Jeremiah:

Jeremiah 1:4-9 states:

"then the Word of the Lord came unto me saying, Before I formed thee in the belly, I knew thee; and before thou camest forth out of the womb, I sanctified thee and I ordained thee a prophet unto the nations.

Then said I, ah, Lord God! Behold, I cannot speak: for I am a child.

But the Lord said unto me, say not I am a child: for thou shalt go all that I shall send thee and to whatsoever I command thee thou shalt speak.

Be not afraid of their faces; for I am with thee to deliver thee, saith the Lord.

Then the Lord put forth his hand and touched my mouth. And the Lord said unto me, behold, I have put my words in thy mouth." (KJV)

Dr. Sharon C. Cason

Jeremiah too, felt unworthy, until the Lord touched his mouth. To be available to God and fit for the service of the Lord, we need the Master's touch. Only He knows the rough places we will have to go. He alone sees the mountains that are impossible for us to climb without His help.

So He reaches out and touches us with His loving hand and then and only then, are we reassured that everything will be alright.

Do you need the Lord to touch you?

When our hearts are overwhelmed and we get weary; when we feel as if we want to faint along the way, we are going to need a touch from the Lord.

All I need is just one touch from the Master's hands and I know that all my issues will be cleared up. All I desire is just one touch from His nail scarred hands and all problems will be resolved. All heartaches will vanish away. Then I will be able to lift my hands up in full surrender and say: HE TOUCHED ME!

Dear Jesus, please reach out your hand and touch me. When I am weary, touch me. When I am sad, touch me. When all seems hopeless and lost, please touch me. Let me feel the touch of your hand, then I will be able to understand that this too will pass. Hallelujah! In your name I pray. Amen!

XXVII

I'M COMING UP

"For though the righteous fall seven times, they rise again…" (Proverbs 24:16—NIV)

Maya Angelou wrote a poem called **"Still I Rise"**. She was a poet, an author, historian, playwright, producer, singer, performer and civil rights activist, to name a few.

This poem depicts the plight of African Americans from slavery and beyond, but with careful observation, we can see that the same poem can evoke a different connotation, to be felt spiritually and reverently.

This poem really speaks to my heart; for there have been numerous times when I have felt forsaken and alone, but the tenacity that God placed within me, gave me the ability to come up victoriously.

When I read this poem, I began to think about all the times that life has done its very best to knock us down spiritually. Just when it seems as though things are going well, then some problem, some worry or some care, pushes us back down again.

The first stanza of the poem says—*"you may write me down in history with your bitter, twisted lies, you may trod me in the very dirt, but still, like dust, I'll rise."*

Yes, the African Americans were kept down by injustice and segregation or just plain old evil and bitterness; but what about the spiritual man? What are we doing to our spirit man? He has no color. He has no nationality or creed but he nonetheless, has been oppressed.

Job 32:8 declares: ***"...a spirit exists in mankind and the Almighty's breath gives him insight." (International Standard Version)***

Hallelujah! We have been given a spirit from the Lord, our Almighty God and it is He that directs our way and draws us to Himself.

My soul's greatest desire, is to be who God made me to be; living out my life with confidence and pride. I look at the things that God have created, the sun, the moon, the flowers and the trees. They all rise.

Maya Angelou says in stanza 3 of her poem: *"just like moons and like suns, with the certainty of tides, just like hopes springing high, still, I'll rise."*

The sun rises. The moon rises. The flowers are sometimes bowed low by extreme heat or cold, but they also rise. Trees become bent from stormy winds and rain, snow or ice, but given a chance, they soon rise as well.

Why can't we do likewise? The creature who has been made in the image of God. The one God breathed the breath of life into; why can't we rise? We are the ones with great hopes. We have strong beliefs. We can rise too. When we come up out of overwhelming circumstances, not allowing anything to keep us down, that is when we will rise.

Stanza 4 of her poem asks several questions:

1. Do you want to see me broken?
2. Do you want my head to be bowed down and my eyes bowed lowered?
3. Do you want my shoulders to droop down like teardrops, because my soul is in misery?

These are questions, which we need to direct inwardly. I understand that the African American slave had to keep his head down. I realize that he had to keep his eyes low and I know that his shoulders and back often drooped because of the beating, the torture and the pain he had to endure; but God has placed a spirit within us and are we allowing that spirit to suffocate and die from abuse and neglect as well?

Satan torments us. He tries to break us. He wants us to be bowed down low, but we cannot allow him to gain control over us. We must get up. We must rise up, like the slaves did. We must come up out of that dark, dim prison of doubt and despair. Rise up and let your spiritual man live again.

Stanza 6 states: *"You may shoot me with your words, you may cut me with your eyes, you may kill me with your hatefulness, but still, like air, I'll rise."*

Where are our priorities? We cannot give the enemy the satisfaction of carrying his heavy load. We cannot hold on to past hurts, regrets and disappointments. We cannot let shame control us. Regardless to what others may do or say, our souls must be anchored in Jesus. Do not allow hateful words and ugly looks to bring you down.

Your life is rich in Jesus.

Your future in bright in the Lord.

Your soul should be joyful and at peace.

Let your spirit man come on up out of depression and degradation.

Laugh! cry! shout! Praise God!

Whatever it takes to come out of that dreadful feeling of anguish, do it and come on up where you belong.

Ephesians 4:30 states:

"and do not bring sorrow to God's Holy Spirit by the way you live. Remember, he has identified you as his own, guaranteeing that you will be saved on the day of redemption." (New Living Translation)

I don't know about you but I am coming up. I am setting my spirit man free. Free to breath. Free to hope and free to think again. So many of our spirits have been so subdued that we cannot even hear from God anymore. The spirit man has been grieved, abused and yes, even starved. The African American slaves were also abused, whipped, starved, and raped. Their hopes were dashed in pieces. Their dreams were buried under blood, sweat and tears. Their aspirations were swept away by the constant hopelessness of their current situation. But now, we look at our spirit man. Have we allowed him to think? Have we opened a door for him to enter, thereby connecting us to God, our creator?

The Apostle Paul states in I Corinthians 2:10-14:

"But God hath revealed them unto us by His Spirit: for the Spirit searcheth all things, yea, the deep things of God.

For what man knoweth the things of a man (except) the spirit of man which is in him? Even so the things of God knoweth no man, but the Spirit of God.

Now we have received not the spirit of the world, but the spirit which is of God; that we might know the things that are freely given to us of God.

Which things also we speak, not in the words which man's wisdom teacheth, but which the Holy Ghost teacheth, comparing spiritual things with spiritual.

But the natural man receveth not the things of the Spirit of God: for thy are foolishness unto him: neither can he know them, because they are spiritually discerned." (KJV)

God has given us wisdom freely. What have we done with what God has given to us?

God has placed a spirit of hunger within us; hunger for divine revelations. Have we feed, nourished and satisfied that hunger, with a consistent and constant study in His Word?

How can we rise up?

How can we come up?

How can we excel, if our spirit man is not properly nourished?

The last stanza of the poem reads: *"leaving behind nights of terror and fear, I rise. Into a daybreak that's wondrously clear, I rise. Bringing the gifts that my ancestors gave, I am the dream and the hope of the slave, I rise, I rise, I rise."*

Romans 6:18 declares:

"Now you are free from slavery to sin, and you have become slaves to righteous living." (NIV)

Yes, like the African American slave, we have been set free and now we are leaving behind everything that is not pleasing to God.

I Peter 2:16 states:

Live like free people, and do not use your freedom as an excuse for doing evil. Instead, be God's servants." (NIV)

I'm coming up. I'm leaving behind the past hurts and fears. Won't you join me?

Dr. Sharon C. Cason

Dear Jesus, my Savior,

Forgive me for grieving your precious Holy Spirit. My heart's desire is to come up where I belong. I want to come up to your holy standard. I want to come up to a life of righteous living. Please continue to go with me as I take this journey of faith. Thank you.

XXVIII

THE SPIRIT OF THE PATRIARCHS AND PROPHETS

We as God's people need great spiritual examples to follow. We need to know that someone has experienced the same things that we have. God did not let them down and neither will he let us down. The Patriarchs and Prophets were men of outstanding quality, some who suffered amid the threat of losing their life but they still obeyed God.

Hebrews 11:32-40 reads:

"And what shall I say more? For the time would fail me to tell of Gideon, and of Barak, and of Samson, and of Jephthah; of David also, and Samuel and of the prophets.

Who through faith subdued kingdoms, wrought righteousness, obtained promises, stopped the mouths of lions, quenched the violence of fire, escaped the edge of the sword, out of weakness were made strong, waxed valiant in fight, turned to flight the armies of the aliens.

Women received their dead raised to life again: and others were tortured, not accepting deliverance, that they might obtain a better resurrection;

And others had trial of cruel mockings and scourgings, yea moreover of bonds and imprisonment; they were stoned, they were sawn asunder, were tempted, were slain with the sword; they wandered about in sheepskins and goatskins; being destitute, afflicted, tormented.

Of whom the world was not worthy; they wandered in desserts, and in mountains, and in dens and caves of the earth. And these all having obtained a good report through faith, received not the promise. God having provided some better thing for us, that they without us should not be made perfect." (KJV)

In these men of God, we see true faith that endured to the end. In them, we see champions of hope and crusaders of a just cause. We see, perseverance and persistent faith that outlasts any affliction or any form of torture. They grabbed a hold of the promises gained through accepting God's Word and sovereign leadership.

First of all, let us take a look at Noah. According to Genesis 6:9:

"Noah was a just man and perfect in his generation, and Noah walked with God."(KJV)

Noah's generation was morally wicked and corrupt but through all of the temptation to pursue sinful pleasures, Noah decided that he was going to be different than the rest, so instead of following the crowd, he began walking with God. Noah followed the pattern that God had laid out for his life.

We know that Noah was a man of faith because Hebrews 11:7 declares:

"By faith Noah, being warned of God of things not seen as yet, moved with fear, prepared an ark to the saving of his house, by the which he condemned the world and became heir of the righteousness which is by faith," (KJV)

The scripture tells us that Noah moved with fear. Noah was given a task to do that seemed impossible and ridiculous. He had to build an ark on dry land and at the same time tell anyone who would hear him that it was going to rain. What? Rain? Certainly Noah had to be out of his mind, because it had never rained before.

Genesis 2:5,6 affirms:

"...for the Lord God had not caused it rain upon the earth...but there went up a mist from the earth, and watered the whole face of the ground."

Noah had persistent faith, he never neglected the task that God had assigned for him to do. His works spoke for him. He not only believed God but he acted on what God told him despite the ridicule and humiliation he had to endure.

Noah had a spirit of like unto Christ Jesus. As Christ humbled himself and became obedient unto death, so Noah was obedient in all that God told him to do, even if it meant death.

Noah was known for his continual faithfulness. He never wavered in his faith, not even 120 years later. His connection with the Almighty God made him strong in faith, power and patience. As a reward for his faithfulness, God saved his entire household.

How can we as Christians today, pattern our lives after the Patriarch Noah?

1. When God speaks to us to fulfil a purpose or plan, like Noah, we must move with fear and reverence, trusting in God alone.
2. We must humble ourselves before God as Noah did, and allow Him to use us, imperfections and all.
3. We must remain faithful in all that we do for God, despite mal treatment or lying tongues.

Next, let us consider another man of faith, called Abraham. According to Hebrews 11:8:

"By faith Abraham, when he was called to go out into a place which he should after receive for an inheritance, obeyed and he went out, not knowing whiter he went." KJV)

Abraham was instructed by God to leave his home and country. God separated him from his family and called him out. Abraham did not question the leading of God, but obeyed, not knowing where he was going. From Abraham, there was no question as to where he was going, all he knew was that he had a direct call from heaven and he did not hesitate to obey that calling. (Genesis 12:1-5)

God promised Abraham that he would make of him a great nation. That He would bless him and then make his name great. Abraham clung to the promise of God. His faith was strengthened by the assurance that God was with him. He was called "the friend of God", because he talked to God face to face. Abrahams whole life was a life of prayer. Through his many trials and tests, he was taught submission, patience and endurance.

Abraham honored God and God thereby, honored him. He revealed to Abraham His divine purpose, stating in Genesis 18:17: ***"...shall I hide from Abraham what I am about to do?***

Even the Angels of Heaven, honored Abraham, walking, talking and even eating with this man called the friend of God. Abraham had the spirit of Christ. As Christ interceded on behalf of all sinners, so Abraham, the father of all who believe, instructed his household in righteousness.

God knew that Abraham would obey him, even down to the point of sacrificing his own son. That is why God supplied the ram in the bush, a substitute. Abraham called the name of the "Jehovah Jireh", the Lord will provide.

What lessons do we learn from the life of Abraham?

1. He was a close friend of God. It's one thing to hear from God and to walk with God but to be considered a friend is quite another.
2. He did not hesitate to obey even when the thing asked seemed utterly imaginable. We must realize that God always have our best interest at heart, even when we cannot see the plan or understand the purpose.

Next, we want to take a look at the life of Jacob, Abraham's grandson. (Genesis 25:21-27) Did he follow in the footsteps of his grandfather? Hardly!

Most of us can probably identify more with the life of Jacob than with either Abraham or Noah. Jacob's life was one of ups and downs. He represents the struggles between the spirit and the flesh.

Before he was even born, he struggled with his brother in his mother's womb. Down through his life he was in a state of unrest and unhappiness because of the choices that he made. His life was full of trouble:

1. He cheated his brother, Esau, out of his birthright.
2. He deceived his father with the help of his mother.
3. He had to run for his life from the wrath of his brother.
4. He loved a woman and was deceived into marrying another.
5. He had to work 14 years for the one he really loved.
6. His wives were jealous of each other and there came a conflict between two sisters.
7. His wages were changed 10 times.
8. He had a divine call to return home, but his father-in-law did not want him to leave.
9. He had to sneak away from his father-in-law to avoid conflict.
10. He was afraid to meet his brother because of what he had done.

Despite Jacob's weaknesses and troubles, he without doubt, was a chosen instrument of God. His whole life turned around when he wrestled with an angel all night long. Through this ordeal, Jacob gained strength and victory. He held on until the angel blessed him.

The spirit of Jacob is the spirit of many today. A life of struggles. A life of ups and downs and ins and outs. He was sometimes happy and sometimes sad; sometimes faithful and sometimes not; sometimes full of zeal and other times fighting the devil, wrestling with trials and temptations. Most of Jacob's life, he wrestled with family problems, starting with his brother, then his wives, followed by his father-in-law, then his children.

Through all of this, Jacob held true to God and God worked it all out in the latter part of his life, even preserving his blood line through his son Joseph.

How can this spiritually weak man, inspire us?

1. We can see his struggles and learn that we do not have time to waste, struggling with our desires. We must spend our life time, working for God instead of struggling against Him.
2. Our life cannot be a sometimes life; sometimes praying and sometimes crying. Sometimes serving and sometimes barely making it. No, we need to allow the Almighty hand of God to work on us, as Jacob finally did and learn how to serve God in spirit and in truth.

Now, we want to explore a few episodes form the life of God's divinely appointed deliverer, Moses. (Exodus 3:1-15)

Moses was:

*   A type of Christ, the Savior
*   A divinely chosen deliverer
*   He stands as a prophet, an intercessor, a leader and as a servant of God.

When Moses was born, Pharaoh had demanded that the Hebrew midwives kill all the male children, because he feared that the Israelites would one day rise up against them. Pharaoh also knew that among the Israelites would come a deliverer.

Moses' mother hid him for 3 months and placed him upon the water in a basket. Pharaoh's daughter found him on the water, raised him up in the courts of Pharaoh, where he became a mighty leader and was taught in all the wisdom of the Egyptians.

Moses knew that the riches of God were greater than those in Egypt, so instead of remaining a son of Egypt, he chose to be a son of a slave. Hebrews 11:25 states:

"He chose to suffer affliction with the people of God, rather than have the fleeting enjoyment of sin," (Berean Study Bible)

Moses voluntarily chose God's way for his life. He could have remained in the lap of luxury, but realizing that his true people were suffering, he too chose to suffer.

Being trained in the house of Pharaoh, made Moses a great military commander, but he never felt worthy enough to be God's leader. Moses did not think that he was fit for the task. He gave so many excuses as to why he should not do the job, but in the end, he obeyed God.

- Moses was a man of many weaknesses.
- He was unsure of himself.
- He was quickly distressed because of the children of Israel.
- He was easily provoked.
- He was at times timid and other times angry.

Yet, Moses learned that above everything that he experienced, he had to be obedient. He did not dwell on what others were doing, but he focused his attention on what God wanted him to do.

You see, it does not matter what others do, we have to give account for what we do. Moses learned that he was not punished for the sins of the people but for his own sin. He had to give account to God for what he did, not what the people did. God stated several times that the people were stiff-necked and disobedient, but it was never God's intention for Moses to bear the sins of the Israelites upon his shoulders.

God knew the extent of their disobedience, all he wanted Moses to do was to lead them to the land of Promise, instruct them in the ways of the Lord and guide them through the rough and bumpy paths of life.

Yet, instead of allowing them to learn from God, Moses put himself in their place, took their shame and bore their blame.

Through the life of Moses, we learn:

1. Sin has a price, especially the sins of the leaders.
2. God demands complete obedience, nothing less will do.
3. God's greatest joy is to know that His people are serving Him because they choose too and not because they were forced too.

The next patriarch we want to discuss, is Joshua, the successor of Moses. Joshua was divinely appointed and ordained by Moses. He was given a charge before Israel and was encouraged to be strong and of a good courage for God was with him.

God said to Joshua:

"Moses my servant is dead; now therefore arise, go over this Jordan, thou and all this people, unto the land which I do give to them, even to the children of Israel." (Joshua 1:2—KJV)

God called Moses to the mountain top and no one ever saw him again. Joshua had once waited in expectancy when Moses came down from the mountain, but now, Joshua was just waiting. He had served Moses well. He had been Moses' personal aid and field commander. Joshua was full of the spirit of the Lord and now God was calling him to lead the people over into the land of promise.

Joshua was fearless, he demanded exact obedience from the people. Joshua stirred up their faith by his life, word and testimony. God knew that his people were still stiff-necked but He also knew that Joshua was the man to get them across the Jordan to a land promised to Abraham their father.

God spoke to Joshua and said:

There shall not any man be able to stand before thee all the days of the life, as I was with Moses, so I will be with thee: I will not fail thee, nor forsake thee.

Be strong and of a good courage: for unto this people shalt thou divide for an inheritance the land, which I sware unto their fathers to give them.

Only be thou strong and very courageous, that thou mayest observe to do according to all the law, which Moses my servant, commanded thee: turn not from it to the right hand or to the left, that thou mayest prosper whithersoever thou goest.

This book of the law shall not depart out of thy mouth; but thou shalt meditate therein day and night, that thou mayest observe to do according to all that is written therein: for then shalt thou make thy way prosperous, and then thou shalt have good success." (Joshua 1:5-9—KJV)

Joshua started immediately on the task that God had given him. He went on in the name of the Lord, never taking down and never compromising. He told the Israelites:

"…if it seem evil unto you to serve the Lord, choose ye this day, whom ye will serve, whether the gods which your fathers served that were on the other side of the flood, or the gods of the Amorites, in whose land ye dwell: but as for me and my house, we will serve the Lord." (Joshua 24:15-KJV)

All of Joshua's victories were won by faith in God.

He divided the river of Jordan, by faith.

He marched around the walls of Jericho and the walls fell down flat, by faith.

He instructed the Israelites to be loyal to God, by faith.

He conquered the enemies of Israel, by faith.

He commanded the sun and the moon to stand still, by faith.

His entire life was one of consecration to God. He was always spiritually minded. He was a man of great courage and complete obedience to God.

From the life of Joshua, we learn:

1. To be courageous in all our endeavors for God
2. To serve the Lord and be faithful regardless to what others do.
3. To walk by faith and not by sight. Hallelujah!

Our last patriarch we want to discuss, is Israel's greatest King, David.

David was a great man of God, called a man after God's own heart, but his personal life was stained with sin. He had many great accomplishments. While tending his father's sheep, he killed a lion and a bear. While still a young boy, he killed the giant Goliath. In the court of King Saul, he soothed the king from an evil spirit by playing on his harp.

The women sang and danced saying of David:

"Saul hath slain his thousands, and David his ten thousands."(I Samuel 18:7-KJV)

David stayed loyal to God and kept the commandments, wholly following the Lord with all of his heart. He was zealous in the work of the Lord and recognized his wrong, even crying out to God for help saying:

"wash me thoroughly from mine iniquity and cleanse me from my sin…create in me a clean heart, O God and renew a right spirit within me." (Psalm 51:2,10-KJV)

David knew the mind of the Lord. He knew God's ways and he knew how to repent. He was one who showed great courage and wisdom in the affairs of God but lacked that same wisdom in his own personal affairs.

In all of his ways, good or bad, David knew how to praise the Lord. He appointed singers in the tabernacle to praise God day and night. He brought the Ark of the Covenant back into Israel with singing, dancing and praise to God.

According to many Bible scholars, 75 to 80 of the 150 Psalms are attributed to King David.

In Psalms 8:1 and 3, David wrote:

"O Lord, our Lord, how excellent is thy name in all the earth! When I consider the heavens, the work of thy fingers, the moon and the stars, which thou hast ordained; what is man, that thou art mindful of him?.. (KJV)

In Psalms 19:1 David affirmed:

"the heavens declare the glory of God; and the firmament showest his handiwork."(KJV)

In Psalm 3:3 David declared of God:

"But thou, O Lord, art a shield for me; my glory and the lifter of my head." (KJV)

In Psalms 86:12 David exclaimed:

"I will praise thee, O Lord my God, with all my heart: and I will glorify thy name for ever more."(KJV)

In the great Hallelujah Psalm of praise, 150, David exhorted us to:

"Praise ye the Lord: Praise God in his sanctuary: praise him in the firmament of his power. Praise him for his mighty acts; praise him for his excellent greatness. Praise him with the sound of the trumpet; praise him with the psaltery and harp. Praise him with the timbrel and dance: praise him with stringed instruments and organs. Praise him upon the loud cymbals; praise him upon the high-sounding cymbals. Let everything that hath breath praise the Lord, Praise ye the Lord."
(KJV)

There are many things which we could say about David. He had many flaws and several setbacks, but his life was one of worship, praise, honor and exaltation of God.

From his life we learn:

1. To put God first in everything.
2. To never be afraid to come to God with our weaknesses.
3. To praise the name of the Lord in every situation, whether good or bad.
4. To honor God when others have forsaken Him
5. To understand that truly, God is a forgiving God. Hallelujah!

Looking back over the lives of these great men of God, we see that there is a spirit which was placed in all of them. A spirit of humbleness and submission to the will and way of the Almighty Father.

By examining their ups and downs, we can reach out with a heart of gratefulness that God has recorded these things in his awesome Word the Bible, to teach us when we need instruction, to turn us when we are wrong and to stir us to action when all seems lost.

My prayer for you to day, is that you allow God to mold you into who He desires you to be, as he molded these great men.

Dear God, our Father,

Thank you for showing us your way. Keep us on the path of righteousness and do not let us stray from the truth of your Word. Thank you for putting your Holy Spirit within me and entrusting us with your plan and purpose. Amen!

•

XXIX

FIVE CHARACTERISTICS OF A CONTAGIOUS CHRISTIAN

Webster's Dictionary defines "contagion" as an influence that spreads rapidly.

When an individual is said to be contagious, he or she is labeled as having something on them or in them that spreads rapidly when they come in contact with other people. It could be a disease, a rash or a viral condition, whatever it is, it is prone to be transferred from one entity to another. But the type of contagion I am discussing, is a relative good type. It can be spread from person to person and is subject to, figuratively, turn the world upside down.

Let's take a look at five characteristics of a contagious Christian.

1. The characteristic of a contagious Christian is their **love.** A contagious Christian knows how to love across all color barriers. A contagious Christian has love that reaches out to others regardless of the situation that they are in.

   Jesus stated in John 13:35:
   "by this shall all men know that ye are my disciples, if ye have love one for another."(KJV)

Love can draw the hopeless person, the one who is weary, the one who is weak and the one who feels lost and alone. Anyone can be infected with love. I may not speak your language, nor share the same ethnicity as you but my love for all mankind does not stop me from loving you.

Love forgets the past. Regardless to what you have done to me in the past or what you have said about me in the present, the love that I display to you can reach over the time span of life and melt even the coldest heart.

I Corinthians 13:4-8 states:

"Love is patient, love is kind. It does not envy, it does not boast, it is not proud. It is not rude, it is not self-seeking, it is not easily angered, it keeps no record of wrongs. Love does not delight in evil but rejoices with the truth. It always protects, always trusts, always hopes, always perseveres, love never fails..." (NIV)

We could discuss the subject of love for all eternity and never really comprehend the depth of genuine love; we could search the world over and never find true love; or we could look to Jesus Christ who gave His life for us, who took our place, bore our sin and took the punishment that we deserved and find the greatest love of all time.

Jesus accusers spit on Him. They put a crown of thorns on His head. They beat Him and ridiculed Him. Then they compelled Him to carry His own cross up a hill. There they drove nails in His hands and feet and crucified Him on that same cross. Yet Jesus gave His life to save them all. **NOW THAT'S LOVE!**

We could never, as imperfect human beings, exhibit that same type of selfless love, but we can live our lives in such a way that the love of Jesus permeates every fiber of our being.

2. The second characteristic of a contagious Christian is their **joy.** Nehemiah 8:10 declares:

   "...since this day is holy to our Lord. Don't be sorrowful, because the joy of the Lord is your strength." (International Standard Version)

   Have you ever been in the presence of someone who is happy and bubbly? When they come into a room, their joy can lift an atmosphere of doom and gloom just by the attitude of joy that they possess.

   The joy of the Lord is what keeps you going when all others fall out of the race. The joy of the Lord helps you to see that the glass is not half empty but it is indeed half full. The joy of the Lord makes you strong when others are weak.

   A contagious Christian radiates with the joy of the Lord. My niece, Shelby, was diagnosed with cancer. She fought a good fight and she finished her race with joy.

   Every time I visited her in the hospital, my eyes wanted to fill up with tears. It took all the fortitude I had to keep from crying and wondering why this sweet young girl had to endure such a horrendous disease like cancer. She was so full of life. I never heard her say a mean thing about anybody. I never saw her mistreat any one. This young lady had a smile that said- "everything is okay", even when everything was all wrong.

   After gaining my composure, I walked into her hospital room and she sat up on the bed and said, "hi Auntie". She had this great big smile on her face that made you want to smile too. When visiting her at home, she still wore that smile even while attached to an oxygen machine. She was infected with the joy of the Lord and if you sat in her presence long enough, you would get infected too.

Hebrews 1:9 affirms:

"even thy God hath anointed thee with the oil of gladness above thy fellows." (KJV)

You see, a contagious Christian is not like other people. They can smile through adversity, through pain and misfortune. When you see a person terminally ill with cancer, smiling and laughing, you need to ask yourself—if they can have the joy of the Lord, why can't I? I have my life. I have my health and strength. I have a few pains now and then but that's only light affliction. Why don't I have the joy of the Lord?

3. The third characteristic of a contagious Christian is their **forgiveness.**

    Have you ever met someone who knows how to hold a grudge? Some people have been mad with each other for over 20 years. If we want to be contagious Christians, we must learn how to forgive so that we can be forgiven.

    Let's take a look at the life of Joseph as recorded in the Book of Genesis.

    Joseph's brothers were so jealous of him that when they saw him coming they said to each other—look, here comes that dreamer. They took his coat of many colors, that their father had given to him, off of him and they put Joseph in a pit. They put blood on the coat and lied to their father saying that a wild beast had devoured Joseph, when actually they had sold him into slavery.

    When Joseph was in Egypt, Potiphar's wife lusted after him, falsely accused him and had him thrown in jail. But Joseph forgave her. While in prison, Joseph interpreted the dreams of the chief butler and chief baker. He told the chief butler that he would be restored to his position, but when he is restored, that he should remember him. The chief butler was restored to his position as Joseph had said, but he forgot about Joseph. Yet, Joseph did not hold this against him.

When the butler did remember Joseph, he told Pharaoh about a man in prison who could interpret dreams. Joseph interpreted Pharaoh's dream and eventually became ruler over all of Egypt.

When his brothers came to Egypt to buy corn, Joseph took them in his home. He feed them. He gave them a place to stay and he later revealed himself to them. When Israel their father died, they thought that Joseph would take revenge on them for selling him into Egypt, but Joseph said to them:

"fear not: for am I in the place of God? But as for you, ye thought evil against me; but God meant it unto good, to bring to pass, as it is this day, to save much people alive. Now therefore, fear ye not: I will nourish you and your little ones. And he comforted them and spake kindly unto them" (Gen. 50:19-21-KJV)

Joseph forgave his brothers of everything they had done to him because in the process of being separated from his family, thrown in prison and forgotten about, God healed his heart and made him to see the real purpose in it all.

Can we see the purpose of God through hard trials? Can we hear the voice of God through stormy winds and hurricanes? We need to learn from the lessons of Joseph and be contagious Christians who have mastered the art of forgiveness.

4. The fourth characteristic of a contagious Christian is their **humbleness.**
   Philippians 2:8 states this about Jesus:

"And being found in fashion as a man, he humbled himself and became obedient unto death, even the death of the cross. Wherefore God also hath highly exalted him and given him a name which is above every name. That at the name of Jesus every knee should bow...and every tongue should confess that Jesus Christ is Lord, to the glory of God the Father." (KJV)

If you want to be a contagious Christian, humble is the way.

I Peter 5:5 states:
"God resists the proud but gives grace to the humble…humble yourselves therefore under the mighty hand of God that he may exalt you in due time." (KJV)

Matthew 18:3,4 affirms:
"Except you be converted and become as little children, you shall not enter the kingdom of heaven. Whosoever therefore shall humble himself as this little child, the same is greatest in the kingdom of heaven." (KJV)

James 4:10 states:
"Humble yourself in the sight of the Lord and He will lift you up." (KJV)

You nor I, do not have to wait for anyone to exalt us, because God will in his time, not ours. We need to be contagious Christians and allow the Holy spirit to make us and mold us in the perfect way of God and only then can our Heavenly Father lift us up. We must humble ourselves to God and say---I'm yours Lord, I belong to you. Use me for your glory.

God is looking for humble Christians who can be used to do a mighty work. People who will stand in the gap for lost souls, those who will go out and evangelize, telling the world about a Savior who has already redeemed them from sin. Are you a contagious Christian, who is humble enough to be used by God?

5. The fifth characteristic of a contagious Christian is their **conversation.**

We must make sure that our conversation is holy.
I Peter 1:15,16 states:

"As he that has called you is holy, so you be holy in all manner of conversation; because it is written, be ye holy for I am holy." (KJV)

Ephesians 2:3 declares:
"We have all had our conversation in times past in the lusts of our flesh, fulfilling the desires of the flesh and of the mind, and were by nature the children of wrath, even as others."(KJV)

Ephesians 4:22 affirms:
"put off concerning the former conversation the old man which is corrupt according to the deceitful lusts and be ye renewed in the spirit of your mind." (KJV)

We have all said things which we should not have said. We have had our worldly conversation, but now it is time to get rid of the old mindset and be renewed in our mind.

Proverbs 15:23 states:
"A person takes joy in giving an answer and a timely word— how good it is! (Holman Christian Standard Bible)
A contagious Christian knows how to speak a word in season. A word that will lift your spirits when you are feeling a little low. A contagious Christian knows how to speak the right words at the right time to bless the soul.

Psalm 50: 23 affirms:
"Whoso offereth praise glorifieth me; and to him that ordereth his conversation aright will I shew the salvation of God. (KJV)

A contagious Christ speaks the right words. They speak words that heal and words that make the spirit come alive.

In Titus 2:1, Paul instructed Titus to:
"…speak thou the things which become sound doctrine." (KJV)

A contagious Christian is not afraid to say, yes there is a heaven and we all want to go there but there is also a Hell that we must shun.

A contagious Christian is not just okay. When I ask my sister how she is doing, she says that she is marvelous. She says it so much until when people see her coming, they say, here comes Ms. Marvelous.

A contagious Christian is not just blessed; they are blessed and highly favored.

A contagious Christian knows how to face each new day declaring: ***"this is the day which the Lord hath made; we will rejoice and be glad in it." (KJV)***

Don't just be a Christian, be a contagious Christian!

Don't just be in the Spirit, be filled with the spirit!

Don't just go along and barely live holy, live as if today is your last day and go out with a praise always on your lips.

Each new day presents a challenge but with God's grace, we can overcome any obstacle which Satan may put in our way to block us from receiving what God has for us.

I admonish you to take these five characteristics of a contagious Christian to heart and go out and infect the world with the glory of the Lord. Approach your life with joy and a smile and allow the Heavenly to take control.

Dr. Sharon C. Cason

Dear Jesus,

I know that my life has not always lined up with your Word, please teach me how to be a contagious Christian in all that I say or do. Help me to be a living example of what it means to be Christ-like. Order my steps in your word and keep me on the paths of righteousness for your name's sake. Amen!

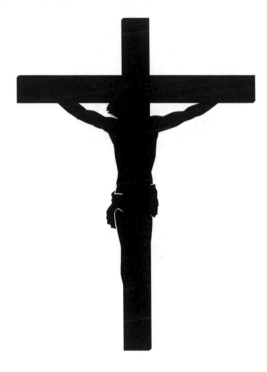

·

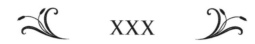 **XXX**

NEVER SETTLE FOR LESS THAN GOD'S BEST

"But covet earnestly the best gifts and yet show I unto you a more excellent way." (I Corinthians 12:31-KJV)

Excellent—means extremely good, outstanding

The synonyms for excellent are: exceptional, superb, marvelous, wonderful, magnificent, terrific, splendid, tremendous, fantastic, or fabulous.

Best—means the most excellent, effective or desirable

The synonyms for best are: finest, greatest, preeminence, supreme, without equal, unbeatable, ideal or perfect.

Phrases used to describe "the best" are: number one, a cut above the rest or second to none.

God has a will, a plan and a purpose for our lives, individually and personally. We are not here by accident. We are not on this earth merely to live for a certain number of years and then die. No! we are here to accomplish a task which God as assigned for us.

No one can be who you or I can be. No one can do what God has given you or I to do. No one can replace you and no one can fulfill God's plan for you or I.

In our reference scripture, the Apostle Paul admonishes us to "covet earnestly the best gifts."

Here Paul uses the word "covet" meaning to yearn to possess or have something. The synonyms for covet are: wish for, desire, crave, hunger after or thirst for.

So in actuality, the Apostle Paul is telling us that we must have a spiritual craving, hunger or thirst for the things of God.

We are to desire the best that God has more than we seek out the best of the world. So many people seek out the best job, the best house on the block, the best car on the car lot and yes, even the best man or woman whom we consider to be the best for us. They are more concerned with having the best that the world has to offer instead of the best that God has already provided.

When Paul says "covet earnestly the best gifts" he is not talking about wanting to be an apostle; wanting to be a prophet or preacher, he is describing the very existence of the child of God.

It is not unbiblical to yearn to have the anointing of a great man or woman of God, but there is so much more to God's best than that.

All the gifts of God are good because they are given by the Spirit of God, but the question is, what gift is best for you?

For many people, life has become a bore. They are bored with life because they have lost sight of who God made them to be and what He designed for them to do.

They are not pursuing their God-given goals. Often times we find ourselves unfulfilled because we are not striving, we are not running and we are not pressing to reach the prize of God, we are just settling.

The Apostle Paul then says, ***"yet I will show unto you a more excellent way"***. There is a more excellent way for us. If we want to succeed in this Christian life, we must pursue that "more excellent way".

In Philippians 3:14, Paul declared:

"I press toward the mark of the high calling of God in Christ Jesus." (KJV)

In Luke 3:24, the words of Jesus are recorded as saying:

"strive to enter in at the straight gate." (KJV)

Hebrews 12:1 admonishes us to:

"run with endurance the race God has set before us." (New Living Translation)

Maybe you have been through tough times. Maybe the enemy has tried to stop you and to block your way. But we must know and understand that he is only fighting us because he knows that God has aligned great things up for us.

Never stop striving!

Never stop pressing!

Move forward!

Satan comes to make you settle for less than what God has intended for you. But I encourage you today, never settle for less than God's best for you.

There are numerous believers all over the world who are unhappy. They refuse to enjoy their salvation or to accept the peace which God has so abundantly provided. A lot of them do not know how to be happy in Jesus alone. They are searching the world for alternatives, substitutes and additives. They need this and they need that. They want this and they want that. It's hard for them to find joy in serving the Almighty God who heals, delivers and sets free. They sit back and they settle.

They settle for a broken heart, when Jesus tells them in His word that He has come **to "bind up the broken-hearted, to proclaim freedom for the captives and release from darkness for the prisoners" (NIV)**

Millions settle for mediocre when the Apostle Paul declared in Ephesians 3:20-21 that God:

"is able to do exceedingly abundantly above all that we ask or think." (KJV)

God has placed more in us than we realize. We must not allow ourselves to sit back and settle for less than God's best. God has greater plans, a greater blessing, a greater anointing and it's all waiting for us.

We should never become content and complacent with average. We must reach for the supernatural. We have more potential and possibilities than we will ever know.

When we are willing to align ourselves with His will, God will bless us more than we could ever imagine.

I Corinthians 2:9 states:

"Eye hath not seen, nor ear heard, neither have entered into the heart of man, the things which God hath prepared for them that love Him" (KJV)

There is a divine design to our lives, one that is destined to be realized. If we could see in the spiritual realm; if our eyes were visibly enhanced to behold the supernatural world, the wonders of God's plan would unfold right before our eyes. We would then suddenly: ***"have power, together with all the saints, to comprehend the length and width and height and depth of His love" (Eph. 3:18—Berean Study Bible)***

A wealth of richness and a world of unlimited possibilities would be ours to grasp.

God has prepared a more excellent way for us.

We have not seen it.

We have not heard it.

We cannot even imagine it.

But it's there.

It is there for the taking. All we have to do is reach out and discover what is best, excellent, desirable, supreme, unbeatable and without equal.

Yes, we do know and we declare; we would shout it to the highest mountain if we were able—***"THAT GOD CAUSES EVERYTHING TO WORK TOGETHER FOR THE GOOD OF THOSE WHO LOVE GOD AND ARE CALLED ACCORDING TO HIS PURPOSE..."(Romans 8:28-NIV)***

Are you called according to God's purpose?

Do you love God?

Then all of those situations and circumstances that you have to endure are working out for your good so that you can perform what God has equipped you to do.

Don't let the evil things that happened in your life, make you bitter towards God. You are stronger than you think.

You can do more than you realize.

You are not falling; you are standing on a solid foundation, which is Jesus Christ, our Lord, our Savior and our King.

If someone has hurt you in life, don't worry. God has more ways for you to experience His joy.

God has a more excellent way.

He has a superb, a splendid, an exceptional way, which has been laid out for you.

Never settle for a little bit of joy when you can have the joy of the Lord that bubbles up and overflows in your life.

Never settle for a little bit of peace when you can: *"experience God's peace, which exceeds anything we can understand. His peace will guard your hearts and minds as you live in Christ Jesus." (Phil. 4:7- New Living Translation)*

Maybe you just have a little bit of faith, but you must use that faith to speak to mountains. (Matthew 17:20)

Okay, you did wrong.

Okay, someone has hurt you, but never sit back and settle for a defeated foe attitude.

I Samuel chapter 30 records the account of the Amalekites and King David at Ziklag. It declares:

Verses 1 and 2--"David and his men reached Ziklag on the third day. Now the Amalekites had raided the Negev and Ziklag. They had attacked Ziklag and burned it, and had taken captive the women and all who were in it, both young and old. They killed none of them, but carried them off as they went on their way.

Verse 3—when David and his men came to Ziklag, they found it destroyed by fire and their wives and sons and daughters taken captive.

Verse 4—So David and his men wept aloud until they had no strength left to weep...

Verse 6—David was greatly distressed because the men were talking of stoning him; each one was bitter in spirit because of his sons and daughters. But David found strength in the Lord his God.

Verse 8--...and David inquired of the Lord, shall I pursue this raiding party? Will I overtake them? Pursue them, he answered. You will certainly overtake them and succeed in the rescue.

Verse 17—David fought them from dusk until the evening of the next day and none of them got away...

Verse 18—David recovered everything the Amalekites had taken, including his two wives.

Verse 19—Nothing was missing: young or old, boy or girl, plunder or anything else they had taken. David brought everything back." (NIV

From this passage of Scripture, we learn that we are to pursue our dreams.

Pursue our plans!

Pursue our destiny!

But whatever we do, never settle!

Do not allow people to define who you are or what you can do.

Pursue your blessings!

Pursue God's best for you!

God has an infinite supply of new mercies and new miracles. He wants to shower all of it on us. Like David, God's plan for us is that we recover all and overtake everything that has kept us spiritual babes for all these years.

We must let His abundant life overflow in us.

We must let His love reign supreme in us.

We must allow the potential that God has put within us to take full control.

God has a magnificent reward waiting for us. A life that's a cut able the rest; success that is second to none.

Never settle for good when you can have God's best.

For years, I settled for good or almost good because I felt that others did not want to see me succeed. I felt that if I give in and just keep the peace, everything will be all right and everyone will be happy. I felt that I had to help others fulfill their desires, rather than fulfilling my own.

I was figuratively, trapped on a bullet train going around and around in circles; on a fast car going nowhere.

I almost reached my goal.

I almost got to the place where, I thought, God wanted me to be; then it was as if the red carpet was snatched out from under me and all of a sudden, I settled, thinking that "well maybe that's not God's will for me." "Maybe God wants me to go in another direction or maybe that is only what I want and not what God wants for me.

I struggled with God's will and my will. Then the Holy Spirit revealed something awesome to me. It was there all the time. I had read the Bible through and through several times, but it was not until I stayed focused on God's will that the revelation became clear to me.

Psalms 37:4 and 5 states:

"Delight thyself also in the Lord and HE SHALL GIVE THEE the desires of thine heart. COMMIT THY WAY unto the Lord, TRUST also in him and HE SHALL BRING IT TO PASS." (KJV)

All of these years, I had delighted myself in the Lord. I had trusted totally in His word and by faith I stood on his promises.

All these years, I had blessed the Lord with all my heart and soul. I had served God with a willing heart and mind.

But there was one thing I neglected to do. I neglected to allow **GOD** to bring it to pass. I neglected to turn it completely over to my Father so that **HE** could give me my heart's desire.

So many times **I tried to bring it to pass. I tried to make it happen.**

Instead of letting God open the door for me, I opened my own door. When presented with a more excellent way, I felt unworthy and unsure of myself, believing that God has not aligned that up for me, maybe it's for someone else. I settled for good-enough instead of best.

That is why I can testify to you today. That is why I can say with confidence and assurance that it is not God's will for you to settle for anything less than His best for you.

I know without a doubt that my Heavenly Father loves me. He has changed my focus and given me peace in my decisions for Him despite any disagreements that I may have to encounter.

I can see God's will for me and me alone, because now I can concentrate on what God has for me.

I am not opposed to helping you to receive greatness but I must not become so absorbed in your mission that I forget what my mission is.

My friends, keep pushing!

Keep striving!

Keep pressing until you reach your goal and never, ever, settle for less than God's best for you.

Hallelujah!

Dear Jesus,

Thank you for showing me where I am weak and giving me the opportunity to come up to your Word. I do not wish to settle for less than your best, so I ask you to condition my mind, refresh my spirit and create a new heart within me. I give you the praise and the glory always.

In Your name I pray. Amen!

CONCLUSION

Fulling the Joy of My Soul

"Is there any encouragement from belonging to Christ? Any comfort from his love? Any fellowship together in the Spirit? Are your hearts tender and compassionate? Then make me truly happy by agreeing wholeheartedly with each other, loving one another, and working together with one mind and purpose." (Phil. 2:1,2-New Living Translation)

"Fulfil ye my joy, that ye be likeminded having the same love, being of one accord, of one mind." (KJV)

"Fulfill my joy by thinking the same way, having the same love, sharing feelings, focusing on one goal." (Holman Christian Standard Bible)

Word was sent to the Apostle Paul concerning the Philippian Church. He greets them in the love of Christ and expresses his concern for them. Paul remembered all that the Philippians had done for him and he was very thankful that God had given them such kindness and grace.

When Paul prayed for the Philippians, he did it with joy. He was extremely happy in his Spirit even while in prison facing a soon execution.

The Philippians had partnered with Paul in helping him to spread the Gospel message through their friendship and financial support. They did not wait to see if Paul would succeed in his endeavors; they knew Paul, they loved Paul and they did not hesitate to support him. They stood beside Paul through the thick and the thin, through trials and tests and in good times and in bad times. This caused Paul to have deep affection for them. They were his heart, his joy and his crown of rejoicing.

It was their love for him that took Paul through every temptation that he had to face and for this, Paul was tremendously grateful.

The Philippians saw, despite many obstacles, that God was still using Paul to spread the Gospel message. Paul knew that the Lord God was in control of his life circumstances even though he was a prisoner.

We are assured that all of Paul's needs were met by the Spirit of the Lord, but God used the Philippian church as a vehicle for those needs. They had been eye witnesses to numerous miracles of deliverance in Paul's life and were certain that the Lord Jesus would continue to be with Paul amid his problems. They did not need to fear; God had always been with them and Paul and He was not about to abandon then now.

So here in chapter 2 of Philippians, Paul continues to exhort them to holy living. He tells them to be of one mind and purpose and to work together wholeheartedly with each other; this Paul said, would fulfill his joy.

It is the joy of every Pastor or Spiritual leader to see God's people walking in love and being holy instruments of the grace of Christ and the love of God.

Paul explains to them that if they have benefited at all from his ministry, then they should be willing to make him happy by continuing in the faith and being rooted in the doctrine that he delivered to them.

In fulfilling Paul's joy, they too would experience joy for their continual abiding in the Word of God.

Like Paul, my joy is full as well. My heart is happy and my love is steadfast; for my Lord, has blessed me and "***has given me the tongue of the learned,***

that I should know how to speak a word in season to him that is weary… (Isiah 50:4-KJV)

I pray that throughout this book of mediation, sermons and inspirational thoughts, that our Father has touched your heart, encouraged you, uplifted your spirit, opened your eyes or just made His Word a little clearer to you than it was before.

I have shared with you the intimate places of my heart and soul, and I pray that you have been nourished by them.

I take great gratitude and pleasure in believing that God has used me as a vehicle for manifold blessings to those who read the words of this book, as he did through the Philippian church to Apostle Paul.

ABOUT THE AUTHOR

As a child, I faithfully attended Mt. Bethel Baptist Church in Virginia Beach, VA., with my family. I was later baptized there as well. As I grew older, my heart and soul yearned for something that I seemed to be missing. But what was it? And How could I get it? I went to church religiously. I sang in the choir reverently. I studied the Bible studiously and I prayed constantly. Yet deep inside, there was a void.

I soon moved to Norfolk, VA, where my husband, our 2 children and I, lived in a small apartment building. As my husband worked the evening shift, I was left alone with our 2 children. One night, when I had put the children to bed, I walked outside to the telephone booth, a few feet from my home, to call my husband. After we were finished with our conversation and I started back to the apartment building, a young lady approached me. She began to talk to me about Jesus Christ.

She asked me if I had received Christ as my Savior and of course my answer was a resounding "Yes I have". I said to her, I go to church every Sunday. I was raised in the church. I study my Bible. I pray, and I added, I sing in the choir.

She explained to me that just because I attended church, read the Bible, sang in the choir and prayed, that, that was no assurance of salvation.

She said that I had to receive Jesus into my heart and then I must live according, to His Word. She informed me, that if I did not do this, then I did not really, love Him at all.

I responded by saying, I love Jesus just as much as anyone. She said, if I loved Him, then I would truly serve Him.

Her words cut deep into my soul for I knew within my heart of hearts that I was not serving Jesus as I should. As she continued to minister to me, she asked me if I wanted to have a personal relationship with Jesus Christ and this time my "YES" was genuine for my spiritual eyes had been illuminated.

I invited her into my home and there we knelt and prayed. I confessed my sins that night and asked Jesus Christ to come into my heart and to live in me; the year was 1977.

Since that night, I have been running for the Lord. I joined the Tabernacle of Prayer for All People under the leadership of Pastor M. M. Terry with Apostle Johnny Washington, of Jamaica New York, as overseer.

I enrolled in the Tabernacle Bible Institute and began to study God's Word with a heart of inner peace and fervor.

To me, Jesus was more than a Savior. He was my comfort, my friend, my guide and my anchor of hope, among other things. The Word of God became alive to me. Never had that ever happened in my life before. As I studied the Bible, God's Word was like honey to me. It was sweeter than apple pie and beyond. I ate and ate and ate and gobbled up, figuratively, chapter after chapter of God's Word, night after night, even reading the entire Bible through and through at least once a year.

It seemed as though, I could not be satisfied. Enough was never enough. I enrolled in Bible College after College. I earned 3 Theological degrees; Bachelor of Theology, Doctor of Divinity and Doctor of Theology, with a concentration in Biblical Interpretation.

Through the years, I continued to study God's Word and grow in the admonition of the Lord. I walked the streets telling people about Jesus Christ. I began teaching, preaching and proclaiming God's Word; offering Jesus Christ to those I encountered.

Later in my life, I opened a Bible School called Center of Joy College of the Bible, in association with International Christian University.

I went from city to city and church to church, teaching God's Word; offering classes for the old as well as the young. Today, that College is growing and the students are hungry and thirsty for more of God's Word. We are enjoying the Lord together and thriving as people of God.

This, my friends, is and has always been, since that night of my conversion, the joy of my heart. I named the school, Center of Joy College of the Bible because Jesus has been and continues to be the **"CENTER OF MY JOY"**. This school has been the fulfillment my heart's joy, which could never be expressed in words.

Many obstacles blocked my way. My path was stained with tears, heartaches, pain and often misery, but I pressed forward to the prize of God.

Fulfilling my joy means that I have reached a stage in life in which what God poured into me, all those years of training in the school of hard knocks and in the desert University, I have continued to pour into students of all faiths.

But now, I have taken it one step further and have etched, spiritually, the words of numerous sermons and inspirations into the hearts of others.

This is what makes me truly happy; being a vessel of honor, clean, polished and ready to be used by the Master.

Through the words of this book, I have fellowshipped with you. I have come into your home. We have tasted of the bread of life together and we have feasted upon the pure honey of God's Word.

During the years of darkness or gloom; during the days of pain or joy and in moments of shear heart felt, soul searching anticipation, we have come to an understanding that what God has imparted to us, can never be replaced.

Be Blessed, My sisters and brothers,
In the Service of the King,
Dr. Sharon Cason BA., DD., THD.

Printed in the United States
By Bookmasters